CULTURE SMART!
FINLAND

Terttu Leney

Graphic Arts Center Publishing®

First published in Great Britain 2005
by Kuperard, an imprint of Bravo Ltd.

Series Editor Geoffrey Chesler
Design DW Design

Simultaneously published in the U.S.A. and Canada
by Graphic Arts Center Publishing Company
P. O. Box 10306, Portland, OR 97296-0306

Library of Congress Cataloging-in-Publication Data·

Leney, Terttu.
Finland : a quick guide to culture and etiquette / Terttu Leney.
    p. cm. – (Culture smart!)
Includes bibliographical references and index.
ISBN 1-55868-842-0 (softbound)
1. Finland–Social life and customs–21st century. 2. Etiquette–Finland.
3. National characteristics, Finnish. 4. Finland–Description and travel.
I. Title. II. Series.
DL1017.L46 2004
948.97–dc22

                                        2004020858

Printed in Hong Kong

Cover image: Fishing boat on the shores of Lake Pyhäselkä.
Terttu Leney

CultureShock!Consulting and **Culture Smart!** guides both contribute
to and regularly feature in the weekly travel program "Fast Track"
on BBC World TV.

About the Author

TERTTU LENEY is a Finnish teacher, trainer, broadcaster, and writer. She currently works for the Foreign Office in London as a professional development coordinator, preparing British diplomats and businessmen for overseas postings. After graduating in Russian and Swedish language and literature from the School of Slavonic and East European Studies, University of London, Terttu completed a postgraduate diploma in language training at the University of Westminster. She has written several publications, including *Teach Yourself Finnish*, *Finn Talk 1*, and *Finn Talk 2*. She lives in London with her English husband and family.

Other Books in the Series

- Culture Smart! Australia
- Culture Smart! Britain
- Culture Smart! China
- Culture Smart! France
- Culture Smart! Germany
- Culture Smart! Greece
- Culture Smart! Hong Kong
- Culture Smart! India
- Culture Smart! Ireland
- Culture Smart! Italy
- Culture Smart! Japan
- Culture Smart! Korea
- Culture Smart! Mexico
- Culture Smart! Netherlands
- Culture Smart! Philippines
- Culture Smart! Poland
- Culture Smart! Russia
- Culture Smart! Singapore
- Culture Smart! Spain
- Culture Smart! Sweden
- Culture Smart! Switzerland
- Culture Smart! Thailand
- Culture Smart! USA

Other titles are in preparation. For more information, contact: info@kuperard.co.uk

The publishers would like to thank **CultureShock!**Consulting for its help in researching and developing the concept for this series.

CultureShock!Consulting creates tailor-made seminars and consultancy programs to meet a wide range of corporate, public-sector, and individual needs. Whether delivering courses on multicultural team building in the U.S.A., preparing Chinese engineers for a posting in Europe, training call-center staff in India, or raising the awareness of Police Forces to the needs of diverse ethnic communities, we provide essential, practical, and powerful skills worldwide to an increasingly international workforce.

For details, visit www.cultureshockconsulting.com

contents

contents

Map of Finland

introduction

Finland has historically been on the frontier between Western and Eastern Europe, between the Swedish Empire and the Russian Empire, and between the Catholic and later the Protestant Western Church and the Orthodox Eastern Church. Today it is an independent, modern Nordic Welfare State. It is a land of great natural beauty, and nature interacts with every facet of Finnish life. Its forests were traditionally a major source of income, but Finland is a world leader in mobile and information technology, and these industries now compete with the paper industry as the main source of wealth for the country. Finland has quickly come a long way from the poverty that was common right up to the 1960s. It is one of the fastest-growing economies in the world, and is a changing society.

Finland's remote geographical situation and the stereotypes of its people have brought about many myths. The *Kalevala*, Sibelius, sauna, *sisu*, and Santa Claus are quintessential elements of what is Finnish, but, as this book shows, the modern reality is complex and more varied.

In fact, it is full of contrasts. The winter days are short, and the summer days are long. The agrarian society of a century ago has become an urban society, which longs for the countryside and retreats to summerhouses every weekend in the season. The ageless natural beauty of the country is reflected in modern Finnish design.

The Finns can be melancholy, but they have a great sense of humor. Their music is often in the minor key, but they love to dance, sing, and perform. They maintain a raft of traditions, from name days to near-pagan rituals—but they are great innovators. They are survivors: if you were stranded on a desert island, your ideal companion would be a Finn. Before you knew it, the sauna would be ready, fishhooks positioned in the sea, a fire burning, and any edible mushrooms and berries picked and prepared for eating.

It used to be said that the Finns have low self-esteem, but this certainly isn't the case today. Young Finns are at home on reality television, joining in great adventures and extreme sports challenges, taking part in pop idol programs, and, of course, backpacking around the globe. Finns return from their travels saying that they live in the best country in the world. The Finnish humorist and writer Juhani Mäkelä advised them to answer the question, "Where is Finland?" by saying, "In the center of the world, of course!"

Key Facts

Official Name	The Republic of Finland, *Suomen tasavalta*. Finland is *Suomi* in Finnish.	A member of the European Union and also of UN, IMF, GATT, WTO, World Bank, OECD, EEA, Nordic Council
Capital City	Helsinki (*Helsingfors*)	
Main Cities	Espoo, Tampere, Vantaa, Turku, Oulu, Lahti, Kuopio, Jyväskylä, and Pori	About 1,000,000 people live in the Helsinki Metropolitan area.
Area	130,500 sq. miles (338,000 sq. km)	Slightly larger than the U.K., Finland is the seventh-largest country in Europe.
Borders	Sweden, Norway, and Russia. Gulf of Finland and Gulf of Bothnia on the Baltic	
Climate	Northern European climate, with cold winters and warm summers	The Gulf Stream brings warmer weather from the Atlantic.
Currency	The Euro (EUR), divided into 100 cents	The Euro, introduced January 1, 2002, replaced the Finn Mark (*Markka*).
Population	5.2 million	65% live in urban areas, 35% in rural areas.
Ethnic Makeup	Majority are Finns, with small ethnic populations of Sami and the Roma	
Details of Other Nationalities	About 65,000 foreigners	Largest groups: Russians, Estonians, Ingrians

Family Makeup	Average household is 2.3 persons. Birthrate falling	High divorce rate; aging population
Language	93% of Finns are Finnish-speaking, 5.6% speak Swedish. Both are official languages.	The Sami and Romany languages are also recognized.
Religion	Approx. 86% Lutheran; 1% Orthodox; 1% other denominations	Approx. 12% of Finns do not belong to any religious group.
Government	Independent republic since December 6, 1917. The head of state is the president, elected for a six-year term.	
Media	Suomen Yleisradio (the Finnish Broadcasting Company) runs the main TV and radio channels. The main commercial TV channel is Mainostelevisio. There are many commercial radio stations. The largest national newspaper is *Helsingin Sanomat*. Many national, regional, and local newspapers and magazines	
Media: English Language	There is a wide choice of satellite/cable television channels. News summaries in English on Web sites of major newspapers	
Electricity	220/230 volts, 50 Hz	Two-prong plugs. Use transformers for U.S. appliances.
Video/TV	Pal B	
Telephone	The country code for Finland is 358.	Code for Helsinki calling from abroad is 00 358 0 + subscriber's no.
Time	2 hours ahead of Greenwich Mean Time; 7 hours ahead of Eastern U.S. Standard time	Daylight saving time (DST) from the last Sunday in March to the last Sunday in October

chapter one

LAND & PEOPLE

GEOGRAPHICAL OVERVIEW

Finland is a land of forests and undulating countryside. The Finns are very proud of their forests, calling them their "green gold." As raw material for the paper and cellulose industries, trees have been, and continue to be, a major source of wealth. They are a renewable resource, and there is more forest now than ever before. Finland leads in the international field of forestry research and sustainable development.

Most of the country is topographically low. The highest hills are in Lapland. Eastern and southeastern Finland are characterized by the large number of lakes, and the west coast is very flat and prone to flooding. The land is still rising after the last ice age. A glacier molded the country during the last ice age, which came to an end only 10,000 years ago; you can see the large granite boulders left behind when the glacier melted.

The total area of Finland is 130,500 square miles (338,000 sq. km). The distance from Hanko on the south coast to Utsjoki in northern Lapland is 719 miles (1,157 km). The longest distance east to west is 336 miles (542 km). Finland is situated in the north of Europe between latitudes 60° and 70° and between longitudes 20° and 32°. The Arctic Circle runs through northern Finland, just north of Rovaniemi, and most of Lapland lies above the Arctic Circle.

Finland shares 381 miles (614 km) of land border with Sweden. The border with Norway is 457 miles (736 km) long. The border with Russia is the longest at 833 miles (1,340 km), and is patrolled by both Finnish and Russian border guards. This border marks the boundary of the European Union with the Russian Federal Republic, and has been the backdrop for many spy novels set in the Cold War era. In the south, Finland borders on the Gulf of Finland and in the west the Gulf of Bothnia, which are both parts of the Baltic Sea. The length of the entire coastline is about 2,860 miles (4,600 km).

Water makes up around 10 percent of the total area of Finland. Forests, mainly pine and spruce, cover 68 percent, and 6 percent of the land is under cultivation, with barley and  oats as the main crops. The remaining terrain includes a great deal of marshy land. There are

187,888 lakes in total, so the name "land of thousands of lakes" is no myth. The 179,584 islands range from small skerries and outcrops to large inhabited islands. Nearly 100,000 of these islands are located in the lakes. Owning an island—or even several—is not unusual in Finland, and every Finn dreams of a house on a lake or by the sea.

Europe's largest archipelago lies off the southwest coast of Finland, and includes the Åland islands (Ahvenanmaa in Finnish), which are an autonomous province of Finland situated between Finland and Sweden. Their status as a demilitarized zone was decreed by the League of Nations in the 1920s. More than 90 percent of the population speak Swedish as their mother tongue.

The largest lake, Saimaa, is situated in southeast Finland. The main Finnish lakes form five long, navigable networks—in fact it is difficult to determine where one lake stops and another starts. There are still some car ferries in the more remote parts of the lakes, but bridges have replaced them in more densely populated areas. It is worth remembering that roads have to go around the largest lakes, making journeys long.

The numerous rivers provide hydroelectric power for the country. Salmon gates have been built on the traditional salmon migratory rivers. There are 5,100 rapids in Finland, the largest being at Imatra on the Russian border. These are now harnessed, but are sometimes released on a Sunday for the pleasure of tourists, and are a magnificent sight. From nearby Lappeenranta you can travel along the Saimaa Canal to Viipuri. If you want to do this trip, ask your travel agent whether or not you need a visa. The canal is leased to Finland by Russia, and runs through Russian Karelia to the Gulf of Finland, providing access from inland lake harbors to the oceans of the world. The city of Viipuri, which was the second-largest city in Finland before the Second World War, was ceded to Russia after the war.

CLIMATE

There are four distinct seasons in Finland, and they are startlingly different from one another. The longest season is winter, when frost and snow turn most of the countryside into a picture postcard. In Lapland the first snow can fall as early as September, and the winter does not come to an end until April or May. In the south the winter is much shorter and milder.

Inland, the country is much colder and drier than the coastal areas. The temperatures in the north can fall as low as -40°F (-40°C). Lakes and coastal waters freeze in the winter, and the ice usually becomes thick enough to support traffic, which considerably shortens some journeys. The snow is at its thickest in March. Large quantities of snow are removed from the city centers to the outskirts for ski tracks and skating rinks. Icebreakers keep the main shipping routes open. The cost of the winter is huge to the Finnish economy.

Spring is dramatic, and can arrive suddenly, the ice on the lakes melting quickly. The summer can be very warm and dry, especially away from the coast, and daytime temperatures can rise to 86°F (30°C). Record temperatures are due to the continental weather coming in from the east. The west wind brings milder, wetter weather. Without the effect of the Gulf Stream, Finland would be a very cold and inhospitable country.

The Finns adore their short, precious summer, and enjoy every minute of it. Cafés spread out on to the streets, beer is consumed in large quantities on terraces, and sun worshipers fill the beaches. The gloriously colorful fall is a very popular time to go trekking in Lapland.

Because the lakes are shallow, the temperature of the water can be as warm as 68°F (20°C), making swimming in the summer a very pleasant experience. However, the Finns also swim in the lakes in winter—a hole is cut in the ice specially for them. This invigorating activity is said to cure many ills, and is certainly not for the faint-hearted! The annual world ice-swimming championships are held in Finland every winter.

The weather is very variable, and talking about the weather is something of a national pastime. Every household has an outdoor thermometer, because it is important to know how much or how little clothing you will need outside. Temperatures can change very quickly. Thunderstorms are common in the summer.

Days are short in the winter and long in the summer. In the north, the Polar night means that the sun doesn't rise at all for several weeks. In summer there is continuous daylight in Lapland for about two months. Even in the south the sun only sets for a short while in midsummer. The magnificent light show of the aurora borealis, or the northern lights (the Finns call them "fox fire"), can be seen on clear, dark nights, on average three out of four nights. The best and most frequent views are from the Kilpisjärvi region, in Lapland, but the lights can sometimes be seen in the south of the country as well.

WILDLIFE

The abundance of water and the warmer weather bring the curse of the Finnish summer: the mosquitoes. These irritating creatures are not so common in towns, but are all the more voracious near lakes and marshes and in the forests, and are particularly plentiful in Lapland. Although these mosquitoes do not carry any diseases, some people have a severe reaction to their bites. If this is the case, seek advice from a pharmacist, who will recommend repellents and ointments. Some Finns swear that beer is the best repellent, but you have to drink large quantities for it to be effective! World mosquito-killing championships are held every summer, the winner being the one who kills the most, using hands only, in a given time. Finns are well practiced at this sport.

There are no polar bears in Finland, contrary to statements made in some guidebooks, but there are brown bears. Most of these are in eastern Finland, but there have been sightings as far south as the outskirts of Helsinki. They present no danger to humans, but can be very bold when they have cubs, and hungry bears are known to kill domestic animals. The ancient Finns worshiped the bear as the king of the forest, and Finnish has more than fifty words for bear—it was believed that you had to refer to him by euphemisms; otherwise the bear thought he was being called, and that was the last thing anyone wanted. Recently, a bear on the runway at Joensuu airport held up domestic flights.

Finns also worshiped the elk, or moose. Some of the earliest cave paintings depict elks, and some of the earliest decorative objects are in the shape of an elk's head. The modern Finns hunt elk. A foreigner wishing to hunt in Finland will need to pass a hunter's test and have the appropriate permit and a Finnish guide. All elk hunters have to wear red or orange hats to avoid shooting each other! The number of permits varies according to the elk population. These large animals are a major hazard on the roads, as are reindeer in Lapland.

There are also many wolves, again predominantly in eastern and northern Finland, but frequent sightings occur all over the country. The rarest mammal is the Saimaa seal, found in the waters near Savonlinna and Linnansaari. Wildfowl include ptarmigan and grouse, and bird migration to the Arctic regions provides bird-watchers with plenty to see in the spring and fall. The ornithologists' paradise is Hangonniemi, the southernmost point of Finland, where the birds rest after crossing the Baltic Sea. The migration of the swans is said to have inspired the first symphony of Sibelius.

The Finnish lakes and coastal waters teem with fish. Pike, perch, and pikeperch are some of the most commonly caught freshwater fish, together with different species of salmon, including the vendace, which is caught by trawling.

A BRIEF HISTORY

From Ice Age to Iron Age

Who are the Finns, and where did they come from? Finns were first mentioned by the historian Tacitus in his history of Germany, but there is very little written evidence about them before the Romans occupied the area. It is known that Finnish hunters traded furs with the Germans, who sold them to the Romans.

The migration of Finnic peoples can be traced through linguistic loans and similarities with other peoples around the eastern Baltic, along the Volga River in Russia, and all the way to the areas around the Ural Mountains, where languages related to Finnish are still spoken. There are many peoples, including the Estonians, the Ingrians, the Votyaks, and others, who share a linguistic past with the Finns. With modern DNA analysis it has been established that the Finns share around 75 percent of their genes with the Europeans of the Baltic region, and only about 25 percent of the genes come from the East or are of Asian origin. The Hungarian language is also remotely related to Finnish.

There are still many unanswered questions about the Finns and the Sami people. Did the Sami people, who now speak a language related to

Finnish, speak some other language before? Who were the Battle-Axe people, and what language did they speak?

Archaeological finds would indicate that the first people—probably hunter-gatherers—arrived in Finland around 8000 BCE, some time after the end of the last ice age. We don't know who these people were, or what language they spoke. The area may have been populated before then, but the glacier would have destroyed any evidence. New finds are being made, and historians may have to reassess the prehistory of the area.

The Finns moved to the area that is now Finland from the south, across the Gulf of Finland, and from the east, along the Karelian Isthmus. There was also some migration from the east coast of Sweden to the coastal areas of western and southwestern Finland along the gulf of Bothnia. The Åland Islands were also inhabited very early. All these areas are still predominantly Swedish-speaking.

There have been some very interesting prehistoric finds in Finland, including some spectacular cave and rock paintings. In addition to the archaeological finds, there are the tales of the *Kalevala*, which tell the story of the heroes of the North fighting battles and carrying out feats of power and intelligence.

The pagan Finns had their own gods. The chief god, Ukko, remains in the language as the word for thunder. Many place-names refer to sacrificial grounds and burial places. Modern methods of research and scientific analysis are constantly revealing more about the past.

The Vikings traveled through Finland on their long journeys to the East. The ancient trading routes still exist, mainly the Kuninkaantie, the King's route, which passes through southern Finland from Stockholm via Turku and on to Russia. Parts of this are a heritage trail today.

From First Crusade to Grand Duchy

More is known about Finland after the Northern Crusades reached the country. Christianity probably arrived in Sweden with Irish monks. The first crusade to Finland took place in 1155, according to legends dating from the end of the thirteenth century, led by St. Henry, the bishop of Uppsala, and King Eric of Sweden.

The papal power was extending its reach from the west; meanwhile the Orthodox faith was actively converting from the east. Sweden wanted to secure the area of Finland, not just for the Catholic Church, but also politically as its frontier toward the east. Ever since then, Finland has been between these two interest groups. The western Finns aligned with the Catholic Church, and the Karelians in the east with the Orthodox faith prevalent in Novgorod, the predecessor to the state of Russia.

The emerging Swedish state tied Finland closer to itself, the first documentary evidence regarding Finland as a part of Sweden appearing in a papal document in 1216. Sweden built fortifications in Häme, Vyborg, and on the south coast. Vyborg Castle, built in 1293, still stands, and is now in Russia. Castles were also built in Turku and Savonlinna, both of which still stand.

In 1323, under the Treaty of Pähkinänsaari, Sweden and Novgorod divided Finland between the two kingdoms. Karelia came under the Novgorod rule, and the west and south of Finland remained within the western culture and the Catholic Church as a part of the Swedish state.

Turku became the capital of the Swedish province of Finland. The Swedish legal system, taxation, and other tools of the state were established. The bishop of Turku became the spiritual leader of the country. Finns had a right to send representatives to the Diet in Sweden in the sixteenth century.

The Reformation and the Lutheran Protestant Church were established in Finland, as elsewhere in Scandinavia, in the first half of the sixteenth century. As Sweden's power grew and expanded eastward, Finland increasingly became a battleground, and hunger and wars taxed the population. Swedish controls were tightened, and Swedes held all the high offices of state.

The glory of the Swedish empire came to an end in the Great Northern War (1700–21). Russia occupied Finland in 1714, when Swedish attention was elsewhere. Then followed the so-called period of the Great Wrath, ending in the Peace of Uusikaupunki in 1721, and southeast Finland became part of Russia. Further battles followed, and Russia's sphere of influence pushed ever further west. There were some fledgling feelings for a Finnish state at this time, and some talk of separating Finland from Sweden. The university in Turku was the center of intellectual activity, but there was still a long way to go before Finland was ready to be a nation-state.

During the reign of Gustavus III (1771–92), there were some improvements in Finland. Work started on the fortification of Viaborg, just outside Helsinki, now known as Suomenlinna. This fort has been attacked only once—by the British during the Crimean War.

This was a period of renaissance for Finland, with improvements in government and the economy, and new towns founded. Some of the officers involved in the war against Russia (1788–90) advocated separation from Sweden, but received little support for their ideas.

Napoleon was enlarging his empire in Europe. In 1807 he met Alexander I of Russia in Tilsit, in Poland. They agreed that Sweden should be coerced to join the blockade against Great Britain, and to force Sweden's hand Russia attacked Finland. This war (1808–9) is known as the War of Finland. The fictional description of the war by Johan Ludvig Runeberg in his narrative poem "The stories of Ensign Ståhl" inspired the Finnish romantic movement, which in turn fueled the nationalist movement of the nineteenth century. The Russians defeated the Swedes, and occupied Finland.

Tsar Alexander I was eager to secure the defenses of St. Petersburg, and it was important to have Finland as part of Russia. After the peace was agreed to in 1809, Alexander I came to Finland and opened the first session of the Finnish Diet in Porvoo. The Finns swore allegiance to Russia, and in return were allowed to keep their Lutheran faith, constitutional laws, and rights established during the Swedish reign. Finland became part of

Russia as an autonomous Grand Duchy. Alexander I was a constitutional monarch, and his representative in Finland was a governor-general. The Finnish senate was established with a four-estate Diet. For the first time, Finland had the machinery of a state. The Tsar favored a strong Finland to weaken Sweden further.

Helsinki became the capital of Finland, and grew rapidly. Viipuri, which had been established as a trading town during the Hanseatic League, flourished, and became the most cosmopolitan town of the Grand Duchy. It was said that many of the citizens of Viipuri were fluent in four languages—Russian, German, Swedish, and Finnish.

From Grand Duchy to Independence

There was growing interest in establishing a Finnish identity. Elias Lönnrot gathered and recorded in writing the oral traditions of poetry and mythical tales of Finnish heroes, which later became, under his editorship, the *Kalevala*. The publication of these epic verses added to the nascent pride in the Finnish language. The subject of language went through bitter disagreements, throughout the eighteenth century and into the nineteenth, between the supporters of Swedish and those of Finnish. This language issue still has echoes in today's Finland. Fueled by Runeberg's

patriotic poetry and by the philosophy and
practical achievements of senator Johan Vilhelm
Snellman, the first Finnish-language
schools were established in the 1860s.
Finnish was also established in the
university system as a teaching
language. This in itself led to great
innovation and work on the language.
Words like *tiede* (science) and *taide*
(art) were coined by the innovators of
literary Finnish, the liberal attitude of
Tsar Alexander II making these advances possible.

The Pan-Slavist movement under Alexander III
and Nikolai II led to measures to diminish the
rights of the Finns. Political freedoms were lost,
but arts and literature flourished. The Golden Age
of Finnish Art received international acclaim at
the Paris World Exhibition of 1900, where Finns
had their own pavilion for the first time. The
composer Sibelius had become world famous, and
his *Finlandia* the anthem of Finnish nationalists.

The turning point in the Russo-Finnish
relationship came after Russia suffered heavy losses
in the Russo-Japanese War. The unrest in Russia
spread to Finland. The Finnish Diet went through a
radical reform. The four estates were replaced by a
unicameral parliament, and universal suffrage was
established, Finnish women being the first women
in Europe to be granted the right to vote.

The Civil War

In the second decade of the twentieth century the Russian grip tightened further, and Finnish autonomy was severely restricted. In Finland, Russians were given equal rights with Finns by law, and political activity was closely monitored by the Russian authorities. Among many Finnish activists, the senator P. E. Svinhufvud was sent to Siberia. He later became president of Finland. The First World War and internal political turmoil in Russia culminated in the Russian Revolution in 1917 and the end of the power of the Tsars. In Finland the senate under the leadership of Svinhufvud made a declaration of independence on December 6, 1917. The Soviet government, led by Lenin, recognized Finland's independence a month later. A bitter civil war followed in Finland. The opposing forces of the left, known as the Reds (landless rural workers and factory workers), and the right, the Whites (the aristocracy, army, and bourgeoisie), some of whom had been trained as the Jaeger battalion in Germany, fought a bitter war that left deep divisions in Finland for a long time. The Whites, led by Carl Gustav Emil Mannerheim, defeated their opponents, and a victory march was organized in Helsinki in May 1918. Mannerheim became the temporary head of state. There were some moves to establish a monarchy in Finland, but under the new constitution Finland became a republic. In 1919 K. J. Ståhlberg was elected the first president. In the same year alcohol was prohibited, and this prohibition lasted until 1932. In 1921, certain tenant workers gained the right to buy their land.

By this time Finnish culture had been further established by the continued success of Finnish arts and literature. Finns were successful at the Stockholm Olympics with Hannes Kolehmainen winning three gold medals in running. The Finnish-language weekly *Suomen Kuvalehti* was founded, and the news agency Suomen Tietotoimisto was established.

Between the Wars

In the 1920s the young republic started to establish its institutions. Education was made compulsory, and both Finnish and Swedish became official languages. National Service was started in 1922. Right-wing tendencies grew, leading to conflict with the left-wing parties, and many arrests of prominent socialist politicians followed. The right-wing Lapuan Liike movement was established in 1929.

The 1920s brought light entertainment, ranging from cinema to jazz and tango, into the country. Gramophone records sold in large numbers and the Finnish Broadcasting Company, Yleisradio, was set up. Women were allowed to join the civil service. Commercial aviation started. At the end of the decade, Finland plunged into depression following the Wall Street crash.

The 1930s saw more antisocialist measures. The right-wing "blackshirts" kidnapped the president; the unrest culminated in the so-called Mäntsälä rebellion in 1932, after which the right-wing activity was curtailed but not eradicated.

The Finnish film industry went from strength to strength. Architecture saw the seminal work of Alvar Aalto in the Viipuri Library, finished in 1935. Some of the rifts caused by the civil war were starting to mend.

The growth of the power of Germany and the looming possibility of war cast a shadow on the general air of optimism that had spread in Finland. In 1939 Frans Emil Sillanpää won the Nobel prize for Literature, and the summer Olympics were due to be staged in Finland in 1940. The Olympic stadium was completed.

The Winter War

Russians wanted to establish military bases on some of the islands in the Gulf of Finland to protect Leningrad. Negotiations were long and unsuccessful. Russia attacked Finland on November 30, 1939. The short, bitter war finished on March 13, 1940. The winter was exceptionally cold, and the losses were heavy. Karelia was lost to Russia, and the Karelians were all evacuated to Finland. The peace was short-lived and the so-called Continuation War started on June 25, 1940. A truce was declared in September 1944.

Early in the Second World War, the German forces occupying Norway crossed over to Lapland in an attempt to sever Allied supply lines to Leningrad. In 1944–5, the German troops still in Lapland retreated, devastating and burning most of the country, including the capital, Rovaniemi. The Paris Peace Treaty of 1947 ordered Finland to pay heavy war reparations to the Soviet Union and to cede the Karelian Isthmus and part of Lapland to the Soviet Union. The Karelian refugees were housed all around Finland. Rationing continued until the 1950s. The return of the soldiers from the front resulted in the biggest baby boom in Finnish history in the years 1945 to 1950.

Postwar Finland

In 1948 the Treaty of Friendship, Cooperation and Mutual Assistance was concluded with the Soviet Union, and this agreement was discontinued only in the early 1990s, when the Soviet Union disintegrated. President Paasikivi established the so-called Paasikivi Line, which continued with his successor Urho Kekkonen. The reparations had forced the Finnish economy to undergo a regeneration and radical change. The Olympics of 1952, held in Helsinki, established Finland on the international map, and to top the success of the year the legendary Finnish beauty Armi Kuusela was crowned Miss Universe.

Finland joined the United Nations in 1955. In the same year the Nordic Council with Sweden, Denmark, and Norway was established, creating a free-trade area. In foreign policy the line of neutrality and nonalignment was actively promoted by President Kekkonen. Finland joined EFTA as an associate member and signed a free-trade agreement with the EEC.

Coca-Cola and rock and roll arrived toward the end of the 1950s. Finnish design came into world prominence with names like Tapio Wirkkala, Kaj Franck, Timo Sarpaneva, and Antti Nurmesniemi. Marimekko was founded by Armi Ratia. Alvar Aalto was a world leader in architecture. *The Unknown Soldier*, a pacifist novel about the war by Väinö Linna, became a huge success, and was made into a film that broke all box-office records.

Politically, the start of the 1960s saw a chilling of Finno-Soviet relations, culminating in the Note Crisis of 1961 over the nomination of one of the candidates for the presidential elections. President Kekkonen continued in office through the whole decade. The Finnish economy grew. There was monetary reform, one new mark replacing one hundred old marks. Forestry and the paper industry, together with shipbuilding and the metal industry, flourished. The baby boomers were squeezed out of the country to the cities, and Helsinki continued to grow. Finland became closer and closer to the rest of Europe.

Culturally, the decade was marked by the blasphemy case against the novelist Hannu Salama and his description of Jesus in *Juhannustanssit*; the book was banned. A second television channel, TV2, started in Tampere; "Let's Kiss," the Finnish dance, made the world pop charts; and the Beatles and Elvis competed in popular music charts with the Finnish tango. Left-wing radicalism was popular among students and artists. One of the main events of the decade was the staging of *Lapualaisooppera*, the musical retelling of the fascist movement of the 1930s. The University of Tampere, which became the leading university for media and social studies, was founded. The Pori Jazz Festival and the Kaustinen

Folk Music Festival were started. There was a change of generations in architecture with Dipoli completed by the Pietilä husband and wife team. The comprehensive school system was adopted. The 1968 French students' revolt reached Finland with the occupation of the Student Union House in Helsinki. The liberalization of attitudes also resulted in mid-strength beer becoming available from supermarkets and shops. Finns took to bingo, and started to travel to the Mediterranean sun on package tours. Even the language changed, with the use of the informal address, *sinuttelu*, replacing the formal, *teitittely*.

The economy moved into recession by the mid 1970s due to the global oil crisis, and migration to the cities and to Sweden continued. Finland became established in the international arena as a nonaligned, politically neutral state, though there were accusations, particularly from Germany, that Finland was under the control of the Soviet Union. "Finlandization," as a term, came into existence. The OECD conference was held in Finland, finishing with the signing of the Helsinki agreement. In internal politics, the period was marked by the birth of many protest parties. The biggest of these was the SMP, or *Suomen Maaseudun Puolue*, led by Veikko Vennamo.

The national lottery came into being, and Lasse Viren won gold medals in the Munich Olympics.

The first-ever rock festivals were held in Turku. The Savonlinna Opera Festival was revived by Martti Talvela. New Finnish operas were composed by Joonas Kokkonen and Aulis Sallinen.

The economy continued to grow, and went through the heady yuppie years. The Metro was built in Helsinki. Environmental issues came to the forefront, the Ministry of Environment was set up, and the Green movement became a political party. The mutual aid agreement with the Soviet Union was extended by twenty years in 1985, but it was annulled in 1992 following the collapse of the Soviet Union. Women could be ordained, but only after a long debate in the Church. Equal rights legislation came into force and a new law on surnames made it possible for women to keep their surname on marriage. Many women went back to using their maiden names, or combined their maiden and married names. The state monopoly on broadcasting came to an end, and the first commercial radio stations started up. The long-term president Urho Kekkonen died in 1986, marking the end of the postwar years.

The 1990s witnessed the economic crisis precipitated by the fall of the Soviet Union and the end of oil barter trade. A banking crisis followed in Finland, and the state had to intervene to safeguard the savings banks.

Unemployment reached record levels. Finland applied to join the European Union, and a referendum was held in 1994 with 56.9 percent of Finns voting for joining and 43.1 percent voting against. The split between urban and rural Finland was marked, with urban Finland voting "yes," and rural areas voting "no."

The national highlight of the decade was in May 1995, when Finland won the world ice hockey championships in Stockholm. The Finnish telecommunications company Nokia led the whole world in mobile telephone technology. The Finnish economy grew very fast. Moving into the twenty-first century, Finland is becoming very well established in the European Union. There is continuing debate in Finland about the pros and cons of joining NATO.

GOVERNMENT AND POLITICS

Finland is a sovereign parliamentary republic. The original constitution came into force in July 1919,

and there were no major changes until the year 2000. The constitution lays down the rules for the highest organs of the state and the constitutional rights of its citizens. The ultimate power is vested in the people, who elect 200 representatives to the Finnish parliament. These elections take place in March every four years, and the electoral system is direct and proportional. The parliament traditionally has representatives of many parties.

In the March 2003 parliamentary elections the seats were divided as follows:

Center Party of Finland	
(Suomen Keskusta) 55	
Social Democratic Party of Finland	
(Suomen Sosiaalidemokraattinen Puolue) 53	
National Coalition Party	
(Kansallinen Kokoomus) 40	
Left Alliance	
(Vasemmistoliitto) 19	
Green League	
(Vihreä Liitto) 14	
Swedish People's Party in Finland	
(Suomen Ruotsalainen kansanpuolue) 9	
Christian League of Finland	
(Kristillisdemokraattinen puolue) 7	
True Finns	
(Perussuomalaiset) 3	

After the elections in 2003, the leader of the Center Party, Anneli Jäätteenmäki, formed the new government, but a scandal connected to leaking information concerning the war in Iraq forced her to resign in the early summer of that year. For a short period Finland had an elected woman president and an elected woman prime minister, the first country in Europe to do so. Matti Vanhanen of the Center Party succeeded her in June as the new prime minister. His government is a coalition of ministers from the Center Party, the Social Democrats, and the Swedish People's Party of Finland. The Center Party had been in opposition for the previous eight years.

Finland has a strong tradition of coalition governments and consensus politics. The welfare state is on the agenda of all Finnish political parties. Women are strongly represented in the Finnish government. There are currently eight women in the cabinet of eighteen ministers, and seventy-six of the current members of parliament are women. The prime minister is selected by the parliament in an open vote according to the new constitution of March 2000.

The presidential elections are held every six years. The maximum period for one president is two consecutive terms of office. Tarja Halonen became the first woman president in March 2000, and is the eleventh president of Finland.

The president, together with the government, forms the Council of State. The prime minister proposes the ministerial posts, and the president officially appoints the cabinet of at least twelve, but no more than eighteen, ministers. The council of state has executive power and the parliament legislative power.

Local government elections are held every four years in the fall. Each municipal authority has a local council with extensive powers, including local taxation, hospitals, health centers, town planning, welfare, and education. The state assists local authorities from central funds. Finland has 446 local authorities, 111 of which are towns (2003 figures). There are plans to merge local authorities to form larger administrative areas. Regional government is divided into five regions, led by the regional governor. Åland has its own local autonomous government.

Foreign policy is led by the parliament and the president. The duties of representing Finland in international affairs are divided between the president and the prime minister under the amended constitution.

In 1999 Finnish voters elected sixteen representatives into the European Parliament for a five-year term. Finnish is an official language in the European Union. Finnish MEPs included Ari Vatanen, the 1981 world motor-rally driving champion, and Marjo Matikainen-Kallström, a many times cross-country skiing world champion. It is not unusual for sportsmen and pop stars to go into politics in Finland. Antti

Kalliomäki, the Minister for Finance, is a champion pole-vaulter, Lasse Viren, the four-times Olympic gold medalist, is a member of parliament. The Minister for Culture, Tanja Karpela, was a Miss Finland.

Finns have traditionally been very active voters, but young Finns today are less interested in politics than in single-issue movements and environmental organizations. There is also an increasing number of small splinter parties, for instance parties representing old-age pensioners.

FINLAND AND ITS NEIGHBORS

Until the early nineteenth century, Finland's role in history was to be the battleground for supremacy between Sweden and Russia. Since its independence in 1917, Finland has clashed with the Soviet Union, but has had a peaceful coexistence with Sweden.

Estonia is regarded as a special neighbor by the Finns. Even though Finland shares a border with Norway, the remoteness of the border area means that there is much less contact with the Norwegians. The Sami people inhabit the area of northern Finnish Lapland, northern Norway, Sweden, and Russia, and have a Sami Council, which promotes their affairs across the whole area.

Self-Definition
A famous Finnish nationalist summed up the
Finnish feelings about their neighbors when he
said, "We do not want to be Russian, we cannot be
Swedish, so let us be Finnish!"

There is a love-hate relationship between the
Finns and the Swedes. Finns like to tell jokes about
the Swedes and the Russians. Seven hundred years
of providing soldiers for the Swedish army, and of
paying the Swedes heavy taxes to run the
administration, left their mark. The lean years
of the Finnish economy forced large numbers of
Finns to move to Sweden to work. Finns were
regarded as second-class citizens in the early years
of this migration, but now that Sweden has large
numbers of immigrants Finns are more highly
regarded, and their children have integrated into
Swedish society.

Sports matches between the two nations are
always bitterly fought. The Finns and the Swedes get
along well, though there are sometimes problems
when commercial companies merge—the Swedes
like a wide consultation process, while the Finns
want quick decisions.

The relationship with Russia and formerly
with the Soviet Union is complex. Since the
breakup of the Soviet Union travel has become

easier. The Orthodox monastery of Valamo in Lake Ladoga is a very popular tourist destination for Finns. There are a number of collaborative projects, including the restoration of the library in Viipuri, which is one of the early works of the Finnish functionalist architect Alvar Aalto.

Many Karelian Finns, who lost their homes in the Second World War, vehemently hate the Russians, and dream of having Karelia back. Large numbers of Karelians and many war veterans travel frequently to see their homeland or battlefields in Karelia.

Finns are starting to analyze the Soviet years more objectively, but there is still a long way to go. Many memoirs and diaries, and the opening up of the Kremlin archives, are providing rich material for historians. There is no doubt that the 1950s, '60s, and '70s were a difficult time. Economically the Soviet Union was for Finland a huge and eager consumer market as well as a buyer of industrial machinery. The breakup of the Soviet Union plunged the Finnish economy into a downward spiral, from which it has now fully recovered. Finnish companies are once again expanding into Russian markets. On the political front, the so-called Northern Dimension, or Finland's strategic position as a gateway from the EU to Russia, is much discussed.

THE FINNS TODAY

The population of Finland passed the 5,200,000 mark in 2002. Today nearly 80 percent of Finns live in urban areas. At the turn of the nineteenth century nearly 90 percent lived off the land. The social and economic changes have been enormous, and the move to the cities means that 0.9 million Finns now live in Helsinki and the adjacent cities of Espoo and Vantaa.

The average life expectancy of a Finn is 77 years. The demographic pyramid resembles that of most other industrial countries, with the middle-aged group predominating. The "baby boomers" of the postwar years are nearing retirement age. Nearly 86 percent of Finns belong to the Lutheran Church, and just over 1 percent to the Finnish Orthodox Church.

Finland also has a Sami population of 6,500, who speak several different dialects of the Sami language, and who traditionally herd reindeer. There are also Sami people living in northern Norway, Sweden, and Russia. Tourism is now a very important source of income. Winter tourism to Lapland has increased with trips to visit Santa Claus, who lives there, according to the Finns! Lapland is also growing in popularity as a destination for skiing and trekking.

The profile of the Sami people has been significantly raised in the last couple of decades with the Sami Parliament and the University of Lapland. Sami culture has gained in popularity, with such artists as Wimme and the folk group Angelin Tytöt singing modern versions of a traditional Sami singing style, *joiku*. There is also a newly found fascination with shamanism. There is an outstanding issue between the reindeer-herding Sami people and the Finnish state over landowning rights.

Only about 90,000 foreigners live in Finland, around 17,000 of whom are refugees. Most of the foreigners have moved there to work, to study, or to marry a Finn. The largest group is the Russians, then the Estonians, and then the Swedes. Refugees from Somalia number around 5,000 and other large groups are people from the Balkans and the former Soviet Union, Iraq, Vietnam, and Germany. By international comparison the numbers are small, but the monocultural Finland of old is moving toward multiculturalism. The influx of new people, the increase in numbers of Finns working abroad, and the general trend of globalization are all having an effect on the Finns and Finnish culture. It is also good for the Finnish gene pool to have an injection of new genes.

Agriculture, forestry, and the construction industry provide a livelihood for 12 percent of the population. Communications and transportation employ 8 percent of the work-force. Financial services and commerce between them account for 27 percent of the employment market. Industry provides work for 21 percent of the population (forest products 26 percent, consumer goods and other manufactured items 31 percent, and metal and engineering products 43 percent). Miscellaneous services account for the rest of the 32 percent. Over 70 percent of Finnish women are employed outside the home.

The recession of the early 1990s started to drive a wedge between the well-to-do and those in danger of social exclusion, including the long-term unemployed. Life was good in the heady days of the 1980s welfare state, but the cost was too high. A banking crisis and the worsening economy brought about redundancies and cutbacks in public spending. Old people, young families, and people in sparsely populated rural areas are suffering, and there are regular soup kitchens in some deprived urban areas. Life continues to be very good for those who are employed and can afford child care and health services.

The Nokia Factor

You can't go anywhere in the world without running into Nokia. The telecommunications company has come a long way from its origins as a tire and rubber manufacturer, though it still produces over 600,000 pairs of Wellington boots every year. Nokia is one of the largest companies in Europe, and in the world. It accounts for more than 3 percent of Finnish Gross Domestic Product and around a quarter of the total value of Finnish exports. A global multinational company with its roots in the little town of Nokia, it is almost 90 percent foreign owned, but not everybody knows that it is Finnish. The company doesn't go out of its way to publicize the fact, and many Finns are annoyed with Nokia for what they see as an opportunity lost for advertising Finland.

Underlying the phenomenal success of Nokia is Finland's excellent education system, providing the know-how needed for the research, development, and manufacture of high technology. In Finland the welfare society is in harmony with the information society. Nokia is hugely significant for the Finnish economy. Large numbers of companies provide it with services and components. The small town of Salo, not far from Helsinki, is often now called Nokia City, as most of its inhabitants depend on Nokia for their livelihood. The headquarters are in Espoo. Nokia can even help to catch criminals, as was shown by the recent case of a robbery, when a passerby used her phone to take a picture of the robber, who was then quickly caught by the police.

The Linux Effect

The richest Finn, however, is not employed by Nokia. He is Linus Torvalds, the information technology wizard who is challenging the mighty Microsoft with his Linux computer operating system. This is an open access system, which is constantly being improved and expanded by its users. It is reliable and cheap, is distributed free via the Internet, and is nonprofitseeking. Linus Torvalds has become a cult figure in the U.S.A., where he works for Open Source Development Labs in Beaverton, Oregon. The Linux system is used mainly by companies providing access to the Internet, by large media corporations, and by telephone companies. The most famous U.S. client is NASA. The special effects for the blockbuster film *Titanic* were produced with the help of Linux. To the annoyance of Bill Gates, his hometown, Seattle, Washington, uses the Linux system for its administration. Linus Torvalds is a citizen of the world. He is quoted to have said: "I believe that nationality is becoming less important today, I am happy to be Finnish, but I am also happy to be able to move around the world."

CITIES IN FINLAND
Helsinki

Helsinki, capital of Finland and "the daughter of the Baltic," is a scenic seaside town, situated on the south coast, on the shores of the Gulf of Finland. It was known in the rest of the world by its Swedish name, Helsingfors, right up to the Second World War. The airport is 12 miles (20 km) from the city center.

Helsinki is now a lively modern city, the largest city in Finland, with over a million people living in the greater Helsinki area, which consists of the cities of Espoo, Vantaa, and Kauniainen. There are many beautiful islands. The warm summers

provide a perfect setting for outdoor activities, but in the bitterly cold winters, with icy winds from the open sea, people stay indoors. The statue of Havis Amanda by Ville Vallgren is the symbol of the town and the focal point of many festivities.

Helsinki was founded in 1550 by the King of Sweden, Gustav Wasa. For a couple of centuries it remained an insignificant town, almost dying out at one time, but the annexation of Finland to Russia saw the start of rapid growth and development. The Russian authorities wanted a capital closer to St. Petersburg, and in 1812 Helsinki became the new capital. The old capital, Turku, suffered a disastrous fire in 1827, after which the university was moved to Helsinki. The university is the largest in the country. There had also been a fire in Helsinki a few years before it became the capital, and this spurred the rebuilding of the town, in the neoclassical style, designed by Carl Ludvig Engel. The oldest part of Helsinki is the Suomenlinna fortress, built on a group of islands fifteen minutes by boat from the south harbor. Helsinki grew rapidly through the nineteenth century to become the largest city in Finland, and the twentieth-century migration from the countryside has made Helsinki and the towns surrounding it home for one in five Finns.

The architecture of Helsinki is a mixture of the neoclassical center, the Finnish national romantic style, and modern and postmodernist architecture. One of the latest landmarks is the modern art museum, Kiasma. The Olympic Stadium was built at the end of the 1930s, but, because of the Second World War, the Olympics were not held in Helsinki until 1952. Helsinki is a great ice hockey town, with the new Ice Stadium and the Hartwall Arena. All three venues are also used for pop concerts.

Helsinki has a permanent amusement park, Linnanmäki (open during the summer months only). Korkeasaari Island houses the town's zoological gardens. Seurasaari Island is the home for a large collection of traditional Finnish wooden buildings and lots of red squirrels! In fact, for anybody interested in modern architecture, there is a great deal to see. You will find guidebooks and brochures at the Helsinki City Tourist Office in the beautiful *Jugendstil* building not far from the famous market in the south harbor.

The church in Temppelinaukio, "the rock church," is another famous landmark, together with Alvar Aalto's last building, the Finlandia Hall, where the Conference for Security and Co-operation in Europe was held in 1975. This conference put Helsinki firmly on the international map, with the Helsinki Agreement bringing East and West closer to each other.

Helsinki has a large number of interesting museums and other places to visit. You might start by taking the number 3T tram, which takes you around the main sights. You can get information from the Helsinki City Tourist Office at Pohjois-Esplanadi 19, or from the Internet.

For the artistically and culturally inclined, there is a great deal to see. Some of the best Finnish art is in the national museum of Ateneum and in the many private collections that are open to the public; there are also, of course, commercial art galleries. Clubbing and eating out are excellent, and there are many annual festivals and sporting events. Check the local press for details.

It is convenient to buy a "Helsinki card" when you want to get around the town and see the sights. It comes with a guidebook, and entitles you not only to free travel on public transportation (buses, metro, trains, boats) but also to free entry to all the main tourist attractions and approximately fifty museums. It will also get you reductions on sight-seeing tours, the Finnair airport bus, car rentals, restaurants, cafés, shopping, and various sports and saunas. The card is valid for one, two, or three days. You can travel from Helsinki by boat to Stockholm and Tallinn as well as to Poland and Germany and by train to Russia.

Espoo

This is the second-largest city in Finland, with about 220,000 inhabitants. Situated on the south coast, just to the west of Helsinki, Espoo has a beautiful coastline and much unspoiled natural beauty, including the Nuuksio National Park. The famous King's Road, which connects Stockholm with Finland and Russia, runs through the town. Nokia has its headquarters in Espoo. There is a long history to Espoo, which has its roots in prehistoric settlements from as early as 3500 BCE. The parish church dates from the fifteenth century. Espoo has as one of its centers the Tapiola garden city, which is a model for town planning for architects the world over. Today Tapiola is a leading technology center in northern Europe.

The Helsinki University of Technology is in Otaniemi, near Tapiola. The former student union building, Dipoli, is a masterpiece by Reima Pietilä and Raili Paatelainen. The campus and university buildings are by Alvar Aalto.

Vantaa

Vantaa, situated due north of Helsinki, is most famous as the location of the Helsinki-Vantaa Airport, which has several times been voted the best airport in the world. Many leading high-tech and logistics companies are situated around it. The Finnish science center Heureka is in Tikkurila. Ainola, the museum home of the great Finnish composer Jean Sibelius, is on Lake Tuusulanjärvi. Close to it is another interesting museum—the studio and home of the famous Finnish painter Pekka Halonen, of the Golden

Age of Finnish art. There was a very lively bohemian artistic population around the lake at the turn of the twentieth century.

Tampere

Tampere, 109 miles (175 km) north of Helsinki, is situated in the region of Häme, on the banks of the Tammerkoski rapids, which run between two large lakes. Founded by the Swedish King Gustav III in 1779, the town is called Tammerfors in Swedish. It was a center for the textile industry, and was one of the birthplaces of the trade union movement in Finland. During the Finnish civil war one of the fiercest battles was fought here. Tampere is now the biggest inland town in the Nordic countries, and the second-largest regional center in Finland after the Greater Helsinki area.

Tampere has two universities, and has produced some of the most famous names in Finnish media and journalism. It is also well known as a theater town. The cathedral was designed by Lars Sonck, and its murals are by the Finnish symbolist painter Hugo Simberg. Modern art is well represented in the Sara Hilden Art Museum. The city's main library, in the shape of an owl, is by Raili and Reima Pietilä. Lenin, the Russian leader, stayed in Tampere during his exile, and there is a museum dedicated to him. Särkänniemi Adventure Park is the most popular amusement park in Finland.

Turku

Turku (Åbo in Swedish) is the oldest city in Finland, the former capital under Swedish rule, and the regional center of southwestern Finland. It is situated on the banks of the River Aura, close to the Turku archipelago, and is surrounded by beautiful countryside. The "Christmas city" of Finland, Turku hosts the special declaration of Christmas peace on December 24 and many events between November and January. In the summer the rock festival of Ruissalo brings crowds of young people to the town.

Turku has two universities, two schools of economics—one Swedish-speaking and one Finnish-speaking—and many high-tech companies. Traditionally the gateway to the west, the harbor is busy and important. Turku has always been a major commercial center, and its name, in fact, means "market place." It has suffered many devastating fires during its long history. The castle, parts of which date from the twelfth century, and the medieval cathedral are the main sights, but there is also the handicrafts museum in the Luostarinmäki, the only street that survived the great fire of 1827. The tall ship *Suomen Joutsen* is anchored on the river, and is now a museum. There are many art galleries and museums, one of the most interesting being the combination of old and new in the Aboa Vetus and Ars Nova complex.

Oulu

Oulu, in the north, is another important regional town. It is now a leading high-tech center with a thriving university, but its history as the most important tar port in Europe goes back four hundred years. It is the fastest-growing urban center outside the Greater Helsinki area. It is often referred to as Finland's Silicon Valley; its technology village, Technopolis, was founded in 1982.

Rovaniemi

Further north, in Lapland, is the town of Rovaniemi. Burned down by the Germans at the end of the Second World War, it has now been completely rebuilt. The Christmas charter flights, bringing tourists to see Santa Claus, land here.

Lahti

In the south of Finland the city of Lahti has become an important conference center with its new Sibelius Hall, the largest wooden building built in Finland for a hundred years and, surprisingly, the first concert hall to bear the name of Sibelius. The hall is home to the Lahti Symphony Orchestra, led by Osmo Vänskä, who has become a leading interpreter of Sibelius's music. Lahti is also an important winter sports center, with two huge ski jumps, and is the starting point for the 100-kilometer Finlandia ski event every winter.

chapter two

VALUES &

ATTITUDES

SISU

The Finnish word *sisu* spread around the world during the Second World War, when a white-clad Finnish soldier on skis appeared on the pages of the Western press. A small, heroic country was fighting the mighty Russia, and the word was used to describe the courage and determination of the Finns. *Sisu* has also been used to describe the Finnish character and behavior. Dictionary definitions include: courage, pluck, stubbornness, stick-with-it-ness, guts, balls, intestinal fortitude, stamina, nerve, heart, energy, gumption, temper, disposition, obstinacy, obstinate spirit, gall, persistency, perseverance, and pride.

Well, you get the idea. Finland suffered huge losses in the Second World War, but retained her independence. Making war reparations to the Soviet Union was another show of *sisu*. The payments were completed ahead of time! Finns pooled all their resources and staged the summer Olympics in Helsinki in 1952 to show the world that there was a bright future ahead. To crown that proud year, a young Finnish girl by the name of Armi Kuusela became Miss Universe and the mascot of the games. *Sisu* had got them through.

There are still many events every year to test this feature of the Finnish character. The sauna world championships, where the winner is the person who stays the longest in the heat of the sauna—temperatures can be as high as 110°C (230°F)—is a test of guts and pride. Marsh football, where those taking part are playing football up to their thighs in boggy marshland, is another trial. Sitting naked on the top of an anthill calls for a lot of *sisu*. The now famous wife-carrying championships also require endurance. There is a slight loss of national pride in this sport since the Estonians have won the competition for three years running—but are the Finns running out of *sisu*? No! While they have to endure their winters, there is no danger of that. And *sisu* is coming into its own in the extreme sports now so popular with the Finns.

Sisu is also a Christian name, and a brand name too—for sweets, trucks, and icebreakers.

PROUD TO BE FINNISH

Finns are fond of saying, "*On lottovoitto syntyä Suomessa*" ("To be born in Finland is like winning the jackpot in the lottery"). They are proud to be

Finnish, and loyal to their fatherland (*isänmaa*)—which is a positive word. Finns like to travel, but only to return to Finland, and confirm to themselves that they live in the best country in the world—in fact they often clap spontaneously when their plane touches down on Finnish soil.

The cosmopolitan Finns feel at home all around the world, but once they return home they know they can relax. The Finnish Nokia executive can attend to global networks from a portable computer at the summerhouse; minutes later he or she will be pushing the boat out on to the lake to catch some fish for lunch, using centuries-old methods. Then he or she can return to enjoy a *savusauna* (smoke-heated sauna). Finnish folk wisdom abounds in such sayings as "*Muu maa mustikka, oma maa mansikka,*" which reiterate that traveling the world is good, but home is always best.

The Finns have been said to have low self-esteem, but this is now changing fast. The new generation is not as retiring and diffident as the previous generations—though boasting and blowing one's own trumpet are still frowned upon. The Finns constantly seek the approval of others. Foreigners are often bombarded by questions: "Do you like Finland?" "Do you like Helsinki?" "Do you think the Finnish women are beautiful?" "Do you like our food?" Such questions are asked almost as soon as you arrive, even before you have had time to see anything, but if you have prepared a few positive answers, they will be pleased!

Finland is also a country of regulations. Cynics say that everything in Finland is forbidden until you have been told that it is allowed, and there are certainly plenty of signs forbidding you to do things. Sticking fastidiously to rules can be annoying. When you want something done, you may be told, "Sorry, can't be done," with the phrase, "*Meillä on sellaiset säännöt*" ("Those are the rules"). This lack of flexibility has caused some problems in the service industries, and young Finns are now being trained to be more customer-friendly.

Finns like to philosophize and "improve the world." Nature inspires them to ponder the meaning of life, and this connection to permanence is important to them. Hugging trees, drawing strength and inspiration from the beauty of the natural world, is essential. Surrounded by nature, Finns can behave very eccentrically.

The Finns are proud of the *Kalevala* and its heroes. The recent success of the *Lord of the Rings* films has further fueled this fire. J. R. R. Tolkien knew Finnish, and was inspired by the Finnish national epic. Elements of the languages his characters speak are based on Finnish. Finns will proudly tell you that the *Baywatch* star Pamela Anderson has Finnish grandparents, as does the Australian golfer Greg Norman, and that these connections make them honorary Finns.

Finns will tell you that they have always been international; after all, there was a Finnish rector of the Sorbonne in the fourteenth century. They are always disappointed if people don't know exactly where Finland is on the map (even if they themselves could not point to the exact location of all the countries of Africa or South America!). The humorist Juhani Mäkelä advised them, if asked by a foreigner where Finland was, simply to answer, "It's easy to find, it's at the center of the world!"

DEMOCRACY

For the Finns, democracy means both freedom and responsibility. They are conscientious citizens, and voter turnout is traditionally high. They believe that, in order to change things, they have to act. It is indicative of the degree of participation that 80 percent of the Finnish workforce belong to trade unions. Collective pay negotiations are conducted between the central trade union organization, SAK, and the main employers' organization. Individual unions will negotiate the details once the main framework for pay raises and pay conditions has been agreed to.

As part of democracy there is the ingrained concept of meritocracy. You advance in society through your achievements, not through birthright. The key to advancement is education, where there is equal access and opportunity. Finland is, more or less, a classless society. Since the yuppie days of the 1980s there has been an emerging *nouveau riche* section of society with an ostentatious lifestyle that is heavily frowned upon by most Finns. But people still like to know how much others earn, and the annual list of highest earners and taxpayers is eagerly read. Most Finnish lottery winners wish to remain anonymous.

The aristocracy that marked the years of Swedish rule is a thing of the distant past, though the manor houses still stand and the families continue. A small number of Swedish-speaking Finns regard themselves as superior to Finnish speakers and maintain some of the aristocratic customs. Finns are ardent followers of other people's royalty, and stories about the royal houses from Sweden to Monaco sell newspapers. The "new royalty" are television stars and sportsmen and women. These days you can also be famous for being famous, as in the rest of the world.

Finns are keen readers—book sales are high—and they are well-informed about world affairs and politics, being avid consumers of news and newspapers. There are fifty-six daily newspaper titles with high circulation figures—a very large number for such a small population. The democratic decision-making process relies on people being well-informed. Democracy is practiced from early days, school pupils having student councils. Parents are involved in educational decision making. Student politics are still active, though there is growing concern about increasing apathy and a drop in voter turnout. On the other hand, single-issue movements are growing in strength. Young people are particularly active in environmental issues.

EQUALITY

The Finnish constitution guarantees equality to all citizens, including equal rights for men and women. Finland, like the other Nordic countries, is often quoted as the being among the most sexually equal countries in the world. The number of women in public life is comparatively high.

Tarja Halonen became the first woman president in 2000, having already served for many years as the minister for foreign affairs.

The Finnish parliament has a high proportion of women, and so does the cabinet. It is apparent, however, that many of these women are in the fields of social, health, and cultural affairs, while the men are in charge of finance, for instance.

The principles and the reality are not the same. Equal pay has not yet been achieved, and Finnish women earn on average 20 percent less than men. There is an equal opportunities commission that handles complaints. Finnish women are well-educated, hardworking, and financially independent. Having a job and one's own money is the accepted norm for Finnish women, and as long as there is good childcare provision—and this is sometimes hard to find—this enables them to work outside the home. But even with the high levels of education and equal rights, there is still a glass ceiling, and most business leaders and university professors are men.

The statistics for violence against women also make for uncomfortable reading. Rape within marriage was criminalized only in 1994. With all the equality that Finnish women have by right, there are still strong macho elements in Finnish life. Older men would not have been caught dead in the kitchen doing "women's work," but the younger generation shares household chores.

HONESTY

Finland has been ranked for many years, in international comparisons, as the least corrupt country in the world. Very few bribery cases come up in the courts. When Finns make a promise, it will be kept, even if it was made when naked in the sauna.

There are, of course, thefts in Finland, but people are very trusting—except with their bicycles! People don't usually lock their bikes in their own front gardens, but don't leave yours unlocked in a public place! In the smaller towns and in the countryside, people leave their skis leaning against the outside walls of their houses, and nobody would dream of stealing them.

The Finns are so honest with their opinions that they can sometimes appear to be blunt. This kind of honesty goes hand in hand with civil obedience, and the Finns are very law-abiding. They will, for example, wait for the pedestrian light to turn green before they cross the road, even if there are no cars in sight.

COMMUNITY SPIRIT

The welfare society is the cornerstone of the Finnish state. Taxation is high, but people are prepared to pay for social and health benefits and for good education. This support for the welfare state is unwavering, even in times of economic downturn. The welfare society was developed over a relatively short period: before the Second World War there was still a great deal of poverty in Finland. Now, however, the cutbacks in welfare and health services that started in the 1990s have begun to bite, and the plight of the elderly has caused a lot of concern.

Local organizations, and most of the successful Finnish festivals and events, rely heavily on the work of volunteers. This custom goes back a long way. It is traditional for friends and neighbors to help each other in exchange for food, particularly when a house is being built. This was the old rural spirit, and there is renewed interest in reviving it in towns. Residents' associations and other community organizations that bring people together are on the increase.

This community spirit is also evident in the concern for the environment. Finland boasts very high recycling rates, especially for paper

and cardboard—60 percent is recycled. The
children learn to help out, too, doing a share of
the household chores and minding their younger
brothers and sisters.

PERSONAL RELATIONSHIPS

Finns can be very private with strangers, but once
you are a friend, you are a friend for life. Friends are
becoming even more important now that, with the
high divorce rate, the nuclear family is undergoing
radical changes. Degrees of intimacy are described
by the different words for "friend." *Tuttu*, or *tuttava*,
is the equivalent of an acquaintance in English,
ystävä is a friend, and *hyvä ystävä* is a good friend.
Hyvänpäiväntuttavat are people you simply greet.
There is also the extended family, *suku*.

The number of divorces has created a large new
sector of single people in the society. There are
about a million single adults in Finland, and the
majority of these are well-educated men and
women over thirty years of age. Meeting other
people is important to them, and dance
restaurants are good meeting places. Internet chat
rooms are very popular. Since March 2002 same-
sex couples have been able to register their union.

The number of single parents, mainly mothers,
is growing. Many fathers see their children only
every second weekend, or even not at all.

THE CHURCH AND RELIGION

The main religion in Finland is Evangelical Lutheran, and the second-largest Church is the Orthodox Church. First the Catholic Church and then, after the Reformation, the Protestant Church in the west and the Orthodox Church in the east of the country have traditionally vied for influence.

The Nordic countries are among the most secular in the world. The majority of Finns value the Church and use its services in their lives. Over 90 percent of children are baptized and confirmed, and most marriages take place in church, with very few people choosing a civil ceremony. The Church keeps the registers of births, marriages, and deaths, and in return for this pays no taxes to the state. Religious programs are popular on radio and television, but church services are poorly attended. The only times the churches fill up are at Christmas and for special events and masses, like carol concerts and the *Tuomasmessu* on December 21.

There is an increasing separation of Church and state, although the President still appoints the highest Church officials, and parishes are still entitled to levy a tax on all Church members, which is collected along with other taxes. There is an ongoing debate about the role of the Church. Women have been ordained in the Lutheran Church since 1988.

There are some strictly puritanical sects in Finland, especially active in western areas of the country and in the north. Many Finns who left the country for the New World for religious reasons in the nineteenth century came from these areas. Other Churches include the Pentecostal Movement, the Roman Catholic Church, the Finnish Free Church, the Adventists, and the Jehovah's Witnesses.

Finns had their pagan religion, and there has been some renewed interest, particularly in shamanism. Many Finnish place-names are linked to pagan practices and rituals.

ATTITUDES TO FOREIGNERS

You will find that most Finnish people are open, friendly, and interested in who you are and where you come from. There have been relatively few foreigners in Finland until recently. Helsinki is a cosmopolitan city, with a sizable business community including representation by many of the global companies, but foreigners are not so often seen in the rural areas, and newcomers are always noticed in small communities. People may stare at you because you look different, but this is out of curiosity, not hostility.

The state and local authorities work together to help immigrants settle. A special program is drawn up for everybody for integration into society, and Finnish language studies are encouraged.

Some unpleasant instances of racism have occurred in Finland, and these are condemned by most Finns. There are some minor extremist movements that are antiforeigner.

chapter three

FESTIVALS
& CUSTOMS

NATIONAL CELEBRATIONS

Most of Finland's national holidays are of
Christian origin. Finnish Independence Day is the
only one that celebrates an historical event. In
addition to the national holidays, there are many
other days in the year that are marked for cultural
or other reasons.

Twelfth Night

Twelfth Night, or Epiphany (January 6), is a
public holiday. It marks the end of the Christmas
period. There are no particular festivities related
to this day, except in the Church. Most people
take down their Christmas trees on this day.

Good Friday and Easter

Good Friday and Easter follow the Western
Church calendar. Some of the customs related to
celebrating Easter have come from the Orthodox
tradition. On Palm Sunday children go around
with a decorated willow branch wishing their
elders good health, and in return receive

chocolate. *Mämmi*, the traditional Finnish Easter dessert, is eaten alongside *pasha*, the traditional sweet pudding marking the end of Lent in the Orthodox tradition. In western Finland people light Easter bonfires, and children dress up as witches and go from house to house expecting sweets. Finns decorate their houses for Easter, and it is traditional to grow some grass in a dish to symbolize the new growing season. Ascension Day and Whitsun (Pentecost) are also public holidays, the dates varying in accordance with Easter.

The Day of Runeberg
On February 5 the Finns mark the birthday of the national poet, Johan Ludvig Runeberg, and eat traditional cakes named after him.

Kalevala Day
Kalevala Day, also known as the Day of Finnish Culture, is on February 28, marking the original publication of the national epic. A number of events to celebrate the *Kalevala* and the Finnish language take place all over the country.

International Women's Day
On March 8 the Finns celebrate International Women's Day by giving flowers and presents to the women in their lives, in celebration of women and women's rights.

April Fool's Day

April Fool's Day is marked by news stories that test people's credulity.

May Day

May Day (May 1) is a public holiday. It is a combination of student festivities, the welcoming of spring, and traditions of the socialist movement. The celebrations start on the eve of May Day. This is a lively, town-centered drinking festival with elements of carnival—balloons, funny hats, and a lot of noise. In Helsinki, students of the technical university place a student cap on the head of the statue of Havis Amanda to mark the start of the proceedings. Traditionally this day marks the official beginning of spring, originally celebrated on May 14, Flora's Day. Serenading in the spring by local choirs on the morning of May Day is another of the traditions. Political and trade union activists organize town marches followed by political rallies. It is customary to wear your student cap on this day.

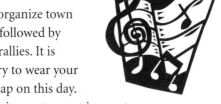

Lunching in a restaurant is a custom, and the menus include a lot of salted fish, to cure the hangovers from the night before!

Midsummer's Day

Midsummer's Day, *juhannus*, falls on the nearest
Saturday to June 21. Midsummer, in contrast to
May Day, is usually celebrated in the countryside.
There is a mass exodus from the big towns. Helsinki
can be very quiet, though traditional celebrations
with bonfires and outdoor dancing are
organized in the Seurasaari outdoor
museum area. As at all Finnish
secular celebrations, a great deal of
alcohol is consumed. Midsummer
is associated with the nightless night,
when the sun doesn't set in the north at
all and only for a little while even in the far south.
The magic associated with midsummer has roots in
pagan fertility rites. Even today maternity wards
experience a peak period in March!

All Saints' Day

All Saints' Day is the first weekend in November.
Candles are placed on family graves on this day
and on Christmas Eve, when they are also put on
all the graves of soldiers who died defending
Finland in the Second World War.

Independence Day

Independence Day, December 6, marks the
Declaration of Independence from Russia in 1917.
A reception is held each year at the Presidential

Palace. The reception marks the climax of the Finnish social calendar, and is televised. The program gets very high ratings. The tabloid press and women's magazines bring out special issues to show pictures of people attending the reception and the dresses worn, details of who arrived with whom, and all the latest society gossip. There are special church services on this day, but it is not a national holiday in the sense of July 4 in the United States.

Christmas

The main Christmas celebrations take place on December 24, Christmas Eve, *jouluaatto*. At noon the traditional Declaration of Christmas Peace is proclaimed from Turku, and most Finns watch or listen to this ceremony on television or radio. The Christmas meal is usually eaten in the early evening, after which families with young children have a visit from Santa Claus. Many sports clubs and charities earn money from Santa Claus appearances. Christmas Day, *joulupäiva*, and the following day, *tapaninpäivä*, are public holidays. Very few public places stay open on Christmas Eve, and nearly all public transportation comes to a halt. Many people now spend Christmas abroad or stay in a spa or a ski resort in Lapland.

New Year's Eve

December 31, New Year's Eve, *Uudenvuodenaatto*, is a big celebration in Finland. Most towns stage a splendid fireworks display at midnight. There are also private fireworks displays, and this is a time for parties and drinking. Restaurants and clubs are crowded. One old custom still practiced by many on New Year's Eve is melting tin horseshoes. The melted tin is cast into a bucket of snow or water, and then the shape is interpreted in the shadow of a candle to predict what the new year will bring.

New Year's Day

New Year's Day is a public holiday. The President makes an annual address to the nation, which is broadcast on radio and on television.

The Finnish flag is usually flown from sunrise to sunset on public and national holidays. At midsummer the flag is flown throughout the night. Individuals can raise the flag for family celebrations, for funerals, and to mark a death.

FESTIVALS

Every July, when Finland is on holiday, there are over eighty major festivals and a huge number of smaller festivals in Finland. There is music, theater, folklore, poetry, dance, and visual arts, along with hundreds of sporting events, from rowing to wife-carrying! The music festivals range from opera at Savonlinna to jazz in Pori, from tango in Seinäjoki to chamber music in Kuhmo.

Many towns in Finland organize an annual night of the arts. These events are extremely popular. The largest event is the Helsinki Night of the Arts, usually held in late August and attended by about two million people. Many of the festivals have

particular associated foods or culinary experiences. In Savonlinna you can enjoy the specialty of fried vendace, the local fish, on Seurahuone Terrace overlooking the lakes on the midsummer night, or a five-course dinner at the Oopperakellari, accompanied by the singers you have just heard at the opera!

Savonlinna Opera Festival is internationally renowned. It takes place annually in the idyllic town of Savonlinna in the lake district. Finnish singers and visiting operatic stars perform a program of operas in the medieval castle of Olavinlinna, on an island in the middle of the town. Each year sees the premieres of new operas here, and these are highlights of the Finnish social calendar.

In addition to opera, the town stages concerts and art exhibitions at other venues. Nokia and other large Finnish companies entertain their corporate clients at the castle and at nearby beauty spots. While in Savonlinna you can visit art exhibitions at the underground art complex Retretti. Also nearby is the famous Punkaharju Ridge, left by the glacier during the last ice age. The Russian Tsars stayed at a nearby villa, now called the Valtionhotelli, which is a hotel and a restaurant. You can get to these attractions by road, rail, or boat from Savonlinna.

Kuhmo Chamber Music Festival, started by the Finnish cellist Seppo Kimanen and his Japanese wife, is one of the world's leading chamber music festivals. It is run by volunteers in the small town of Kuhmo, in the northeast of the country. There is a different theme each year, and over two hundred concerts take place over nine days and nights, with the venues ranging from old schools to the church. The festival made world headlines in the mid-1980s, when the talented Soviet pianist Viktoria Mullova defected to the West while performing at Kuhmo.

Kaustinen Folk Music Festival is one of the longest-running festivals of what has come to be called world music. Musicians from all over the planet come together to hear each other, to teach music, and to spread it to the rest of the world. It is the biggest folk music festival in the north of Europe. There are now many other folk music festivals. One of the up and coming ones is Kihaus, in Rääkkylä, in northern Karelia, started by Sari Kaasinen, the founding member of the Finnish folk rock group Värttinä, who are currently writing some of the music for the musical of *The Lord of the Rings* planned for London's West End in 2005.

Pori Jazz Festival attracts some of the leading jazz musicians of the world, including such artists as the late Miles Davis. The Tango festival in Seinäjoki is the showpiece for Finnish tango. The Helsinki Festival consists of two weeks of music, dance, and theater, all around the town.

FAMILY CELEBRATIONS

Finns mark the rites of passage with established customs. These vary from one family to another, and from region to region.

The christening or baptism takes place when the baby is around two months old, and the name to be given is kept secret until the time of the ceremony. It is traditional to give a child at least two first names, the second often being one that runs in the family. Most people choose names from the official name day calendar, thus giving the child a name day to celebrate. The name day calendar exists for Finnish, Swedish, Sami, and Orthodox names. Even pets have name day calendars.

Celebrating name days is universal in Finland. The day is marked with presents from close friends and family, and lots of congratulatory cards or text messages from others. In the workplace it is customary to mark your own name day by bringing in cakes or sweets to share with your colleagues.

Most people also celebrate their birthdays. A special birthday song is sung to the hero of the day, and children have birthday parties. Once the eighteenth birthday arrives you are allowed to drink legally for the first time, and a pub crawl is customary, with many bars giving a free drink to mark the occasion.

For adults, traditionally only the fiftieth birthday is marked by a big celebration, but increasingly the thirtieth and fortieth birthdays are also marked. You will see announcements of fiftieth birthdays in the local press. Most people hold an open house and receive delegations of relatives, friends, colleagues, golf partners, and members of organizations and societies they are involved with, who come to make speeches and present gifts. Those who do not wish to do this must warn people that they will not be receiving visitors on that day, for instance by placing an announcement in the local press, saying "I will not be celebrating my birthday," "*En vietä syntymäpäivääni,*" or "I will be away," "*Olen matkoilla.*"

As the majority of Finns are members of the Lutheran Church through their christening, the confirmation, usually at the age of fourteen, is marked by confirmation school or camp followed by Holy Communion. Families organize a party, and the godparents are expected to attend. Even though Finnish society is increasingly secular, most couples get married in church. Big weddings are fashionable. The wedding is preceded by hen (women-only) and stag (men-only) parties for the bride and groom respectively—usually riotous events involving dressing up and crazy activities planned by their closest friends to celebrate the end of their single lives. Alcohol always plays a big part.

Wedding anniversaries are celebrated within the family, as also are Mothers' Day, the second Sunday in May, and Fathers' Day, the second Sunday in November. St. Valentine's Day, February 14, is celebrated in Finland as Friendship Day, and cards are widely sent.

The year before they finish upper secondary school, as the top class leaves for the examination season, young people dress up in old-fashioned costumes or formal evening gowns, to let the younger pupils know who is in charge. This day is called *Vanhojenpäivä*, the Day of the Elders. It ends with a formal ball. The outgoing students go around the town on the last school day on floats, dressed up as anything or anyone, from clowns to political figures, with banners proclaiming their feelings about the end of the school year, and making a lot of noise. The idea is that everybody in town knows that they have finished school. This event is called *Penkinpainajaiset*, which, roughly translated, means, "sitting down on the school bench for the last time."

The end of school is celebrated by a ceremony at school, followed by a party with the family, and then the young usually move on to a local restaurant or bar. This is a poignant day for them, heralding as it does the loss of daily contact with their school friends. Money is usually given as a present.

Universities organize doctoral promotions, which are formal affairs followed by a formal ball. Honorary doctorates are also granted at these occasions.

chapter four

MAKING FRIENDS

HOSPITALITY

Hospitality is a matter of honor and pride for Finns. As a guest, even if just for coffee, you are expected to try all the different things on offer. There may be something savory to start off with. Then there could be five or six different kinds of cake, such as buns, coffee cake, or cookies, followed by cream cakes. Allergy and medication are the only valid excuses for refusing anything without offending the host and hostess. The Finnish hostess often doesn't sit down at the table, because she sees it as her duty to ensure that the guest has everything. At the table the guest is served first.

If you are invited to a Finnish home, summerhouse, or sauna, this is an honor, and you will probably become lifelong friends. If you say no, not only do you risk offending, but you will miss out on a real experience.

Corporate entertainment is growing. The large companies take their foreign guests to events such as the opera festival in Savonlinna or the jazz festival in Pori. In addition to the music, you will be treated to some delicious food and often a cruise on the lake or the sea.

If you eat out with a Finn, male or female, you are expected to go fifty-fifty on the bill, unless you were invited by the Finn, who would then expect to pay. If you do the inviting, the Finn will thank you for your hospitality in person next time you meet, by saying, "*Kiitos viimeisestä!*"

CONVERSATION AND CULTURE

Contrary to stereotype, the Finns love talking. When you sit in a café in a marketplace there will be lively conversation and laughter all around you, particularly in the summer. In the winter it is hardly surprising that most people want to hurry back indoors and don't stop to chat for long.

The stories about Finns who don't speak much, or who get annoyed if you talk too much, are mainly myths. Maybe it is simply that foreigners don't like silence. The pace of conversation may be slower than you are used to, and there will be periods of silence—with which the Finns are comfortable.

Although the general Finnish mood may be melancholic, among friends Finns love to laugh, joke, and exchange funny stories. There are strong regional differences. The eastern Finns of Savo and Karelia are more talkative than the people of western Finland. Finns love to philosophize about the world. The best place to do this is at the lakeside, with your toes in the water at the edge of the jetty after a sauna on a summer's night, with long periods of silence—but the silence signifies awe and appreciation of the beauty around you, not that there is nothing to say. The consumption of alcohol releases Finnish tongues.

Most Finns love to talk about sports. So if you want to be popular, take an interest in ice hockey, or Finnish footballers abroad, or the continuing success of Finns in motor sports—but don't mention skiing's recent doping scandals.

Stand-up comedy is gaining in popularity, and the Finns should be naturals at this, as some are more prone to monologue than dialogue. However, most don't want to stand out in a crowd. This shyness is often the reason for the silence in public places. People talking loudly in public are frowned upon or thought to be drunk. That said, the Finns talk loudly on their cell phones. They are keen talkers on the telephone, and sometimes seem to be more comfortable like this than face-to-face!

FORMALITY VERSUS INFORMALITY

Finns are usually fairly informal. It has been said that the new Finnish national costume is the tracksuit. Formal dress or Sunday best is usually fairly understated. There are occasions when the Finn will don a suit, but very few. Finns think nothing of appearing naked with the same sex, whether it is in the sauna (of which more later) or in the changing room of a public swimming pool.

Finns are on first-name terms with all their family and colleagues. Titles used to be important, but are far less so now. In fact many people do not use their titles except on their curriculum vitae or in a professional context. The words *herra* (Mr.) and *rouva* (Mrs.) are not much used, except when the first name is not known, and children call their teachers by their first names. There is a movement toward teaching young people more formal behavior, particularly if they need to deal with their counterparts in central Europe, where the rules are different. Guidebooks with advice on social etiquette and correct conduct have recently been best-sellers in Finland.

ALCOHOL AND ENTERTAINMENT

If you are having coffee in a Finnish home, you may be offered a glass of brandy or a local berry liquor. At the lunch table many Finns drink milk or *piimä* (soured milk). At business lunches drinking is not as common as it used to be. Finns do not drink if they have to drive, and this is an acceptable excuse, as is pregnancy, or being on medication.

After the sauna, Finns will usually offer you a glass of beer, but some people prefer coffee. The local sparkling wine, *kuohuviini*, is drunk at celebrations like birthdays and weddings, but beer and vodka are usually also available, along, of course, with nonalcoholic drinks.

The number of nondrinkers is shrinking, and statistics show that the consumption of alcohol in Finland is rising. The biggest rise has occurred in the consumption of the less strong alcoholic drinks, and soft drinks laced with alcohol—the so-called "alcopops." Binge drinking on Friday nights is common. Alcohol is the cause of 3,200 deaths a year in Finland.

GIFT GIVING

Finns have been brought up never to visit someone empty-handed. The usual gift is a bunch of flowers. There are plenty of florists in Finland, and the selection of flowers is excellent, though they can be expensive in the winter. The florist will wrap the bouquet according to the weather and to how long you need to keep it wrapped, but you should remember that it is polite to take the wrapping off the flowers before handing them to your hostess. If you are going to a formal dinner, you can have the flowers sent. At Christmastime Finns send friends and relatives bouquets of flowers as a seasonal greeting.

Other suitable gifts include glassware, candles, or something from your own country. If you are going to visit friends at a summerhouse, a bottle or two of wine would be a good present.

JOINING CLUBS AND SOCIETIES

Foreigners can join any clubs or organizations they wish, including political parties. You can use all local libraries free of charge, and most of them have a wide selection of newspapers and magazines and access to the Internet.

chapter five

THE FINNS AT HOME

QUALITY OF LIFE

The Finns enjoy a very high quality of life. The environment is clean, and the natural beauty of the countryside offers plenty of recreational opportunities. The welfare state is well-established, and Finland is a very safe place to live, with crime at a low level on the international scale. A bomb blast in a crowded Finnish super-market in the fall of 2002 shocked the Finns very deeply. This sort of occurrence is extremely rare.

Finland has its share of problems. The high suicide rate of young men in particular is often quoted. There are health problems, including heart disease, but the Finns have been very successful at tackling this by educating people to change their eating habits and lifestyles. The North Karelia project for eradicating heart disease is highly regarded in the medical world.

The quality of life is further enhanced by the excellence of Finnish design. The Finns are very particular about their houses and their interiors. The public buildings echo the appreciation of quality and beauty. Finnish design is world famous, with household names including the architect Alvar Aalto, the Hackman design group, glass manufacturers Iittala, and the textile giant Marimekko.

LIVING CONDITIONS

The Finnish winter dictates the standard of the country's architecture. With winter temperatures dropping as low as -22°F (-30°C), houses have to be well-built. The traditional wooden houses of the past have given way to ultramodern buildings with all the modern conveniences. The 1970s saw a boom in house building. Most Finns say they would prefer to live in a detached family house, preferably within sight of a lake or the sea, and close to their workplace. Fifty percent

of houses are such single-family homes. Apartment blocks are almost as popular in town centers, and make up 40 percent of the housing stock. Semidetached houses and terraces, or rows of joined houses, make up the rest of the housing stock. The room area per person is approximately 36 square yards (about 30 square meters). This is a huge change from the prewar years, when large families often shared one room. Housing costs are high, and so are the heating bills.

Town planning is highly developed, incorporating land designated for leisure, special bicycle tracks or light traffic roads, and sports grounds. All Finnish towns are geared to the use of bicycles. Schools, hospitals, and health centers are modern and well-equipped. There is a renewed interest in the remaining old housing stock, and renovating old houses is in fashion.

THE FINNISH FAMILY

The Finnish family has changed radically since the 1960s. Cohabitation is increasingly common. The divorce rate is very high—nearly half of all marriages end in divorce, and there are more unmarried than married adult Finns. The average size of a household is 2.3 persons. The birthrate is low: there are 1.7 children per woman born in Finland. Childless couples are increasingly common. There are over 100,000 single parents with children under the age of eighteen. The aging population also means that more and more old people live on their own.

As a result of divorce and remarriage there are a large number of so-called "neo-families," which are often very complicated, with children and stepchildren. The new surname law that came into force in 1995 allows a woman to keep her maiden name after marriage or use both maiden and married names. Children can be given the surname of either parent or both. A neo-family can have as many different surnames as there are members, and one can barely imagine the complexity of Christmas visits! In this respect Finns are very family-minded, and keep up with the wider family.

In most Finnish families both parents work outside the home, including over 70 percent of mothers with preschool children. Childcare is a major cost for families and the society. Preschool childcare is well-organized, either at municipal day-care centers or in private homes with trained and approved childcare providers. Care in private homes is the most popular, but around Helsinki and some of the other bigger cities there is a shortage of places. There are also private kindergartens. It is now very fashionable to send children to foreign-language kindergartens.

Trace Your Cousins!
Ironically, with the breaking up of so many nuclear families, genealogy is becoming a very popular hobby, helped by a combination of well-kept church records and the Internet. Over a million Finns have left Finland since the "hunger years" of the 1880s, many emigrating to the U.S.A. and Canada. Their descendants, in turn, are seeking their Finnish roots. Cousins are sought and found all over the world, and families have big reunions.

DAILY LIFE AND ROUTINES

Finns are used to working hard: their ancestors eked a living out of a very hostile land. Work is highly valued, and it is by study and work that a Finn gets ahead in society. The Protestant work ethic is deeply ingrained. The average working week is 39.3 hours, and the holidays are generous by international standards.

There is an increasing gap between the "haves" and the "have-nots." Unemployment is long-term, and is particularly high in the remote rural areas and some of the small towns. The average unemployment is around 10 percent. There is a severe shortage of skilled workers in the greater Helsinki area, but there is not enough housing. When the postwar generations retire, Finland will need more workers, and immigration is one obvious possibility.

The working day starts early in Finland. Many factories start at 6:00 a.m. Local authority and state offices open at 8:00 a.m., and the school day starts at 8:00 or 9:00 a.m. at the latest. This also means that babies are taken to day care very early. Most people have breakfast (coffee and porridge, yogurt, or bread) and read the newspaper before going to work. Finns traditionally live close to their workplace, but increasing numbers of people now commute, especially from the Greater Helsinki area.

Because of the early start, lunch begins at 11:00 a.m. or 12 noon, and the evening meal is usually served around 5:00 or 6:00 p.m., particularly in families with children. Many people have their main meal at lunchtime, and only a snack in the evenings. Formal dinners are served at continental time, usually starting at 7:30 or 8:00 p.m. Finns do not go visiting late at night or make telephone calls after 8:30 in the evening, unless they know it will be acceptable.

Finnish food is very similar to the food of other northern European countries. Meat, particularly pork and beef, and fish are standard fare, with potatoes. Sausages, *makkara*, of various sorts are also popular. The many regional specialties include Karelian pastries, *karjalanpiirakka*, and the fish pie of the Savo region, *kalakukko*. Berries and mushrooms, either gathered from the forest or cultivated, are also typical fare. Convenience foods are growing in popularity.

Finns eat a great deal of bread, and drink a lot of milk. They also drink more coffee than any other nation in the world—over 24 pounds (11 kg) per person each year. They drink it in the morning, in the afternoon, in meetings, after the sauna, at weddings, and at funerals. When you visit a Finnish home, the coffee is put on right away. Finns are very particular about their coffee, and the beans are roasted in Finland to suit the Finnish taste. Most of the coffee is imported from Colombia and Costa Rica.

Finns take their shoes off when they come into the house. This is a custom that they take with them when they go abroad, and they are surprised to find that it is not a universal habit. Other Scandinavians do so, and the Japanese, of course. A foreign visitor would not be expected to do so, but if you want to go native on this, the gesture would be appreciated. This is a custom in the home, not in public places. It is done for a practical reason—with the weather being what it is, the wet, mud, and dirt of the outdoors are confined to the hallway, keeping the rest of the house clean. When attending a concert or going to the theater in the winter, women, particularly, will carry with them a pair of indoor shoes to change into when they leave their coats at the cloakroom. Again, this is a practical matter, as the boots needed to negotiate the slippery and icy streets are too hot to wear indoors.

The Sauna

The sauna is a sacred place for the Finns. Sauna is an almost religious cleansing ritual for the body and the soul. When a Finn builds a house or a summer-house, the sauna is the first room to be finished.

There are over two million saunas in the country, and there are many different types. The traditional smoke-heated *savusauna* is regarded as the ultimate experience, and there are still many of these, but modern convenience means that most saunas are now electrically heated. The ideal location is by a lake, so that you can cool off in the water between sessions of sitting in the steam created by throwing water on the hot stones of the stove. Business negotiations are often carried out at company saunas, and this practice has meant that women have often been excluded from decision making as unisex saunas are not the norm. Public saunas as such have disappeared, but you will find a sauna at all swimming pools, good hotels, and spas.

If you have never had a sauna before, get a Finn to show you what to do, and don't be afraid to try the famous birch twigs—they feel very pleasant and are good for the circulation. Drinking alcohol in the sauna is not a good idea, but a beer after it is wonderful. It is advisable not to eat before a sauna, but a good meal to follow it is a part of the ritual. Remember to cool down well, and you will feel relaxed and cleansed.

If you are staying with a family you will find that the women go to the sauna first, with the children, and the men afterward. Sometimes couples go together, but mixed saunas are only for very good friends. Sauna and sex do not go together. If you are visiting Finland in the winter, you could try swimming in the frozen lake, in the special hole made in the ice, or rolling in the snow. This is very invigorating.

THE SUMMERHOUSE

The urbanization of Finland is a postwar phenomenon, and many Finns still yearn for the countryside. They are prepared to drive long distances to escape the town in the summer, and are not put off by the traffic jams out of Helsinki on Friday and back on Sunday. July is the main holiday month, and it is often said that the whole country is on vacation then. When Finland joined the EU, where most of the other member countries have August off, there had to be some adjustments to match holidays with European colleagues.

The rural retreat is often a summerhouse in the region of the old family home. There are 400,000 summerhouses, most of them located next to a lake, on an island, or by the sea. Each has its own sauna, of course. With the increase in numbers of people working from home, and the Internet, many Finns are converting their summerhouses for all-year-round use. The exodus from country to the towns has not been reversed, but the stress of modern living has made many think again. The Protestant work ethic has its price, and burnout is a common consequence of stress. Working from the summerhouse could be a solution.

Typically, the summerhouse is more primitive than the town dwellings. Finns like to get back to nature. President Koivisto was quoted as saying that his best form of relaxation is cutting firewood at his summerhouse. The current president, Tarja Halonen, is a city girl, but when she was Minister of Foreign Affairs she relaxed at her allotment, and she hasn't given up her allotment just because she is now the president.

If you are visiting Finland and want a real Finnish experience, don't refuse an invitation to a summerhouse. If no such invitation is forthcoming, you can rent one.

ATTITUDES TO CHILDREN

Finland is a child-friendly country. Public services are geared to children being with their parents. Bank lobbies have play areas, and there are special carriages on intercity trains with play facilities. If you fly to Finland with Finnair, families with young children are boarded first, and children are given activity packs. Most Finnish restaurants have children's menus and high chairs for toddlers.

A small nation regards its children as its most important resource for the future. Medical welfare starts before birth. All families are given a maternity pack with everything the baby needs for the first few months of its life. Provisions for maternity and paternity leave are good.

The high divorce rate has caused a sharp rise in single-parent families. The courts usually grant the mother custody of the children, and there is growing concern about the absence of fathers in children's lives and the psychological effect of divorce on children. There are also concerns about latchkey children, and after-school clubs are a help here. Sometimes parental guilt leads to children being spoiled, as money and material goods are used as compensation for absence, and there have now been two or three generations of children who are used to getting everything they desire. Children's rights are taken very seriously and there are many events each year on the Day of Children's Rights, November 20, which marks the declaration of children's rights by the United Nations.

SCHOOLS AND EDUCATION

The Finnish education system scores highly in international comparisons, coming top not only in exam results, but also in terms of cost per student. Fifty-six percent of the population have completed postprimary education, and 13 percent have university degrees or their equivalent.

Compulsory education is free, and together with science and culture receives around 18 percent of Finland's budget. Local authorities are responsible for arranging general education, with aid from the central government. Preschool provision is available for six-year-olds, and compulsory education starts in the year the child reaches the age of seven. The school year is divided into two terms, each having a week's holiday in the middle—a fall break in October, and a skiing holiday in February or March.

Finnish children are independent from an early age. When the school year starts, in mid-August, it is common to see children learning their routes to school. After this they are not usually taken to school by their parents, but make their own way, and this is a matter of pride for the children. In the sparsely populated countryside, there is free transportation to school if the journey is longer than five kilometers (just over three miles). School journeys are the bread and butter of many rural taxi drivers!

The schools are comprehensive, with nine compulsory years and an optional tenth year. The school system is divided into the junior level (years 1 to 6) and senior level (years 7 to 9). The aim is to provide a socio-ethical and aesthetic education in addition to the traditional subjects of Finnish, Swedish, or Sami (according to the child's mother tongue), and mathematics, history, geography, and foreign languages. Everybody has to learn Finnish, Swedish, and English. Good schooling is the basis of the Finnish knowledge-based society. Education is held in high regard, and is the source of social mobility. In the junior schools children learn all their subjects from one class teacher, except for languages, which are taught by specialists. At the senior level teaching is done by subject specialists. Teachers are trained at universities.

The reading skills of Finnish schoolchildren were highest in an OECD study in 2002. The most significant background factor is the interest of the young people and their enthusiasm for reading as a pastime. The high level of professional skills of teachers, the use of information technology, and the strong Finnish reading tradition are also contributing factors to this achievement. Textbooks are beautifully produced. Finland has a long tradition of high literacy, and its library services are excellent. Finns are great readers in general and very eager newspaper readers. Over 60 percent of fifteen-year-olds said that they read a newspaper regularly as well as magazines and comics. Young people are avid users of e-mail, cell phones, and the Internet. It is also thought that the subtitling of television programs strengthens reading skills.

School food is free for all in compulsory education. Young people are provided a balanced, nutritious diet, and details of school menus are available to parents on the Internet.

Most young people stay on in education until the age of eighteen. At sixteen they either continue in the three-year upper secondary schools or follow courses in vocational schools, the length of the courses varying from two to five years. Upper secondary school is modular. Many of them specialize in a variety of subjects from arts to sports. Study grants are available.

Matriculation examinations happen nationally twice a year, in spring and in fall. Those who wish to go to university must pass these, and most universities also have entrance examinations. It is hard to gain admittance. Each year more young people apply to universities than there are places. Many continue in vocational schools or vocational universities, in which education is available for most trades and professions. After the longest specialist courses students are qualified to apply for university places. This is a very long route to university.

After school the majority of Finnish boys enter national service before going to university or joining the labor market. The minimum length of service is 240 days. Girls can enter national service if they wish, but few do.

There are nearly twenty universities and art academies in Finland. Since Finland joined the European Union, an increasing number of Finnish students are studying abroad. The U.K. and Sweden are the most popular destinations, and some students go to the U.S.A.

Universities are state-owned, and controlled by the Ministry of Education, but self-governing. The average length of university studies is four to five years. There is funding from state grants or state-guaranteed loans, and the state also subsidizes student accommodation, health care, and meals. There is an attempt nationally to match the subjects studied to the demands of the labor market. More and more emphasis is put on science and technology, and Nokia and other Finnish high-technology companies have a constant supply of very highly educated employees. Most universities offer the chance to study and take examinations in English to encourage foreign students to come to Finland. Research and development is funded by both the state and the private sector. Particularly, technological research is considered paramount to keep Finland at the forefront of global technological innovation. Philosophy, Finno-Ugrian languages, social sciences, forestry, and mathematics are also internationally important. Medical research, particularly into coronary diseases, cancer, and diabetes, is renowned. Open access to higher education is through the annually held summer universities.

Finns are committed to continuing education, and this is provided to adults by local authorities, trade unions, volunteer organizations, and folk institutes in a variety of subjects. Lifelong learning continues also in the workplace. Retraining courses are available for the unemployed and to people who are in professions and trades that are changing or disappearing. The Open University is also growing. There is a good free library provision to support studies at all levels. In e-learning, Finns are at the leading edge in the world. The Virtual University operates in cooperation with state radio and television.

If you ask Finns what they consider to be the most important factor for getting ahead in life, most would say that it is education. Finland's economic success is very largely due to the successful education system.

TELEVISION AND RADIO

Nearly all Finns—96 percent—have a television. Around 80 percent have access to satellite television through cable or satellite dishes. Nearly 70 percent have video or DVD recorders. The television system in Finland is Pal B. Only a Pal B system or a multistandard television will work there, and this also applies to video recorders. There are lots of video rental shops with a wide range of English-language videos, as they are always subtitled. Sports and news are mainstays of Finnish television, and the evening news at 8:30 p.m. is a focal point; it is also the social cutoff point—you don't call or visit people after this time. Television also includes a large number of soap operas, domestic, British, and American.

All foreign-language programs are subtitled. The two national stations, TV1 and TV2, are run by the Finnish

Broadcasting Company. The commercial stations are MTV3 and the privately owned Nelonen. There are a number of local television channels. There are both state and commercial radio stations broadcasting in Finnish, and some in Swedish.

RENTING PROPERTY

Real estate is advertised on the Internet. All the necessary information, including prices and pictures of houses and apartments, is available on the Web pages of real estate agents. There are show apartments in new developments; details will be in the local press or on the Web sites. If you wish to rent vacation accommodation, this too is available on the Internet, but you can also pick up brochures from travel agents or the Finnish Tourist Board.

APPLIANCES

The electric current in Finland is 220 volts, 50 Hz. Plugs are European two-prong plugs. Most hotel rooms have telephone sockets for modem dialing to the Internet: some have cell phone chargers.

Cooking stoves are electrically operated. Most households have microwave ovens as well as conventional ones. Toasters and kettles are rare. If you are renting, ask the rental agency to specify the appliances that are provided for your use.

chapter six

TIME OUT

SHOPPING

Shopping is regarded as a leisure activity by many urban Finns. There is a great variety of shops and markets to be explored, including modern indoor shopping centers and large, outdoor flea markets. The number of out-of-town shopping areas is growing.

Opening times on weekdays vary, from supermarkets opening as early as 7:00 a.m. to small boutiques opening at 11:00 a.m. Most supermarkets remain open until 7:00 or 8:00 p.m. On Saturdays opening times are shorter and more variable, and some small shops don't open on summer Saturdays. On Sundays small stores can stay open all year-round between 12:00 noon and 9:00 p.m. The larger department stores, the supermarkets, and grocers' shops outside the towns are open on Sundays from June through August, and on Sundays before Christmas.

On Christmas Eve and Midsummer Eve shops close early, and on public holidays all shops are closed.

Finland has excellent modern designers. Artek specializes in furniture by Alvar Aalto and glass by Aino Aalto. Look out for designs by Markku Kosonen in wood, Anri Tenhunen in ceramics, Johanna Gullichsen for linen products, and Ritva Puotila for paper yarn carpets. Marimekko stores are good for textiles.

The main shopping streets in Helsinki are Pohjois-Esplanadi and Etelä-Esplanadi for design products, and Aleksanterinkatu for Stockmann's and other large department stores. Akateeminen and Suomalainen Kirjakauppa are the biggest bookstores, and there are many antiquarian bookshops. You will find art galleries and small shops in the pedestrian area of Iso-Robertinkatu. Itäkeskus, Iso Omena, and the Tapiola center are also well worth visiting. You might like to check out the covered market, situated in the south harbor opposite the Palace Hotel. There you can find salmon—fresh, smoked, and cured—as well as the famous Finnish smoked hams.

In smaller towns the main shops are around the market square and the covered market. In the summer the market square is the center of activities and musical entertainment. Many towns have pedestrianized shopping areas.

BANKS AND CASH MACHINES

Banks in Finland are normally open from 9:00 a.m.
to 4:30 p.m., Monday to Friday, but the hours may
vary regionally and some banks stay open later.
Banks are closed on Saturdays and Sundays. The
main banks are Sampo, Nordea, and Osuuspankki.
There is usually a queuing system for customer
service, and you need to pick up a number on
arrival. You may be asked to prove your identity.
There are plenty of cash machines, usually located
by the banks, in shopping centers, and in some large
department stores. Foreign-exchange offices, open
daily, are located in the Helsinki-Vantaa airport
arrivals hall, around the center of Helsinki, and at
the ports. Larger hotels will also exchange money.

American Express, Diner's Club, Eurocard,
Access, Master Card, and Visa are accepted in
hotels, restaurants, and most shops and
department stores. Many Finns bank on the
Internet. They don't use checks, and most people
don't carry very much cash. Smart cards and
other forms of electronic payment, including
payment using a text message, are common.

EATING OUT

Helsinki is famous for its restaurants—including
its Russian ones—and in fact all the major cities
have a good variety. You can check the up-to-

date listings on the Internet, at your hotel, or at the local tourist information center.

Dining out in the evening is more expensive than eating out at lunchtime. Special lunchtime offers usually include a salad or a soup, a main course, bread, and coffee. Freshwater fish is a Finnish delicacy. Game is also good. Business travelers may wish to keep in mind that restaurants are emptier after 1:00 p.m., if they wish to be able to have a good discussion over lunch.

Finnish menus usually indicate dishes suitable for vegetarians. If you have an allergy, it is best to check the ingredients with the staff. Lactose- and gluten-free dishes are also indicated.

Helsinki has a long tradition of café culture. The first café in Finland, Café Ekberg, opened in 1861 in Bulevardi. It is the most famous of the old cafés, and the cakes and pastries are delicious. Fazer Café, in Kluuvikatu, is also good. For architectural ambience you could try the Café Eliel at the railway station, designed by Eliel Saarinen and recently renovated. Cafe Socis, opposite the station, stays open until the early hours of the morning.

There are few public restrooms. At cafés, you ask for the key at the counter, and there may be a charge. The letter M on the door signifies the men's room, and the letter N is for women.

BUYING ALCOHOL AND DRINKING

The state has a monopoly on the production and
sale of alcohol in Finland, and their outlet is the
Alko stores. You can also buy medium-strength
beer from supermarkets and other stores. Alko
stores open Monday to Thursday, 10:00 a.m. to
7:00 p.m.; Friday, 10:00 a.m. to 6:00 p.m.; and
Saturday, 9:00 a.m. to 4:00 p.m.; but in
bigger towns and shopping centers they
are usually open at the same times as
the shops (9:00 a.m. to 8:00 p.m.
Monday to Friday, and Saturday 9:00
a.m. to 6:00 p.m.). Anyone over the
age of eighteen can buy mild alcoholic
drinks, up to 22 percent alcohol by
volume, for example wine, beer, or

mixed drinks, but you have to be 20 to buy spirits or any other kind of alcohol. You may be asked for proof of age.

Beer is the most popular drink. It come in three strengths: I, III, and IVA or export. Strength I beer or pilsner is virtually nonalcoholic. It is a mystery what happened to strength II beer! Answers on a postcard . . .

Drinking habits differ in urban and rural areas. Wine is more popular in towns, vodka in the country, and the further south you go the larger the selection of wines you will find. The north of the country and the rural areas are faithful to Koskenkorva, the Finnish vodka. It is worth trying the local drinks, for example cloudberry liquor or cranberry vodka. There are a lot of local producers of berry wines and liquors. One local delicacy particularly worth sampling is the Finnish sparkling wine made of white currants.

Finns usually drink to get drunk rather than to socialize. This is particularly true of the Friday-night ritual of getting seriously drunk. There is wide social acceptance of drunken behavior. Loudness when drunk is common in a society that otherwise speaks quietly. It is not only the young who get drunk, and the summer festivals can be very noisy and riotous. Finns are not prone to boasting, but they do brag about the severity of their hangovers.

Restaurants serve beer from 9:00 a.m. and other alcoholic drinks from 11:00 a.m. onward. The service of alcohol ends half an hour before closing time. Some cafés have a license to serve liquors with coffee. There are also a growing number of pubs that brew their own beer.

The "booze cruises" from Finland to Estonia and Sweden are popular. They have two purposes: drinking and fun. Many travelers don't disembark for longer than to buy some alcohol or to do a little shopping. Well-known entertainers appear on the cruise ships, and television quiz programs are broadcast from them.

Alcohol-related health and social problems are serious. While the state enjoys the revenue from the sale of alcohol, it has a responsibility for the nation's health and welfare, and sales are strictly controlled. With Estonia joining the European Union, the future of duty-free alcohol is uncertain.

It is not uncommon to see young people, sometimes even children, very drunk on Friday nights, and this can be disturbing. Alcohol poisoning in Finland is five times higher than elsewhere in Scandinavia.

NIGHTLIFE

Finns enjoy dancing, and are good at it, so a favorite way to spend the evening is to go to dance restaurants. You don't generally expect to eat at one of these, though some serve snacks. There is usually a charge for admission. The music is usually live, and the ladies' evenings, when women ask men to dance, are particularly popular. Traditional dances such as the tango and the waltz are favorites, but the twist, rock and roll, and foxtrot make an appearance. If you want more modern music, head for a disco. Summer dances are organized in special outdoor pavilions.

Helsinki and some of the larger towns have a number of nightclubs, and there are usually one or two in smaller towns. They stay open until late, and some have floor shows.

You stand in line to get into a dance restaurant or a club. The doorman is a law unto himself, and will let you in or not, as the case may be. As you leave the club, don't forget to tip him. You also have to pay a fixed cloakroom fee. Waiting in the Finnish winter is not much fun. The age limit for entrance to a club can sometimes on weekends be as high as twenty-four! Watch out for the dress code. Some upmarket clubs require men to wear a jacket and tie, and don't allow shorts or sandals in the summer.

In the run-up to Christmas, restaurants fill up with office parties—a chance to let your hair down with your colleagues. There is often a program of entertainment, with silly games, singing, seasonal food, and copious amounts of alcohol and dancing. The single-sex prewedding parties are also very loud and boisterous.

British- and Irish-style pubs are popular, and, in the summer, outdoor cafés and beer-drinking venues.

The only casinos are at Ramada President Hotel in Helsinki and at Hotel Arkipelag in Marienhamn, in the Åland Islands.

SMOKING

Finland has very strict smoking laws. Smoking is not permitted indoors in public buildings or other places open to the public, or in areas for customers in businesses, except in bars and restaurants with specially designated smoking areas. Smoking is not permitted at public events, in taxis or on public transportation (though some trains still have small smoking cars), in childcare centers, schools, or other educational institutions, or in offices or other places of work (but employers may provide a designated smoking area). Finnair was the first national airline to ban smoking on all its flights, though airports have special smoking rooms.

People don't usually smoke inside their own homes, but go out of doors or on to a balcony.

SEX AND THE CITY

The Finns are fairly liberated when it comes to sex, and women are as likely as men to take the first step. With the growing number of single and divorced adults, casual sexual encounters are common. Dance restaurants are the places to find company for the evening, and more often than not also for the night. Hitting on the opposite sex is expected. At its shortest, the Finnish man's pickup line is succinct: "Your place or mine?"

Going on vacation without your partner is quite common, and extramarital affairs and one-night stands take place, especially on weekend seminars and work-related courses. The discovery of a partner's unfaithfulness does, however, usually result in divorce or separation. Marriage is a fragile institution in today's Finland.

Prostitution was traditionally not visible in Finland, but has recently reemerged. With equality of the sexes, Finnish women are somewhat surprised at this, and at the popularity of prostitution with Finnish men.

Programs with sexual content are common on late-night television.

COMPLAINING

Finns are reluctant to complain. They don't like potentially embarrassing situations. They will swallow their annoyance, complain to their family and friends, and never return to the offending shop or restaurant. It has been said that Finns would quietly remove a fly from their soup rather than cause a scene. Consumer rights entitle you to return faulty or damaged goods.

HIGH CULTURE

There is a great love of and interest in music of all kinds in Finland, and the country has a very strong tradition of musical education. Sibelius and the opera, particularly modern opera, are famous. Helsinki Opera House is one of the most modern in Europe, and there are numerous classical music festivals and events across the country all year-round. Most towns have several choirs and at least one orchestra, a municipal art museum, and a variety of other museums. Helsinki and Tampere are the most famous theater cities, but all large towns have a municipal theater, and there are many interesting art venues.

Some of Sibelius's contemporaries are being explored and are coming out of his shadow. Aulis Sallinen, Joonas Kokkonen, Kaija Saariaho, and Einojuhani Rautavaara are among the many who made their names in the latter half of the twentieth century, and there are a number of avant-garde composers. Experimental art and music are strong. Most of the world's leading opera houses have Finnish stars, and Osmo Vänskä and Esa-Pekka Salonen are among the many internationally known Finnish conductors.

POPULAR CULTURE

Finnish popular culture is not well-known outside the country. Finnish art cinema is led by Aki Kaurismäki, who was on the shortlist for the best foreign film category in 2003 for his film *A Man Without a Past*. Cinemas show films in their original language, with Finnish and Swedish subtitles. Most major American films are shown in Finland.

Finnish popular music is quite varied. The Finns love the tango, and have developed their own tango culture. The Finnish tango is usually in the minor key, and the words tell of lost love and longing. Each year a popular tango festival is held in Seinäjoki, ending with the crowning of the Tango King and Queen for the year. Certain stardom awaits the winners.

Youth music is international. The leading Finnish heavy rock band is called Nightwish. Rap music, Finnish-style, is popular and the main star is Pikku G. Finnish folk rock is widely known on the world music scene. The band Värttinä have toured the world. Leningrad Cowboys have a cult following, gained by their role in the Kaurismäki movie *Leningrad Cowboys Go America*. Jazz continues to be popular.

Television and radio broadcast all types of light entertainment and music. Names to reach outside the domestic market include Ville Valo of Him, and the dance scene disc jockey Darude.

SPORTS

Most Finnish men and many Finnish women are sports mad, and the madder the sport the more it is liked. Facilities are good, and media coverage of all sports is extensive. There are sports for all seasons. Sailing, windsurfing, and waterskiing can be practiced all around the country. Winter sports are popular, Lapland being the best place for downhill skiing, though there are some very minor hills further south. Cross-country skiing facilities are available everywhere, including Helsinki. You can skate in the open air and in ice stadiums. Golf has grown in the last few years, and there are many excellent golf courses where a visitor may play as a guest. The most enthusiastic players have developed ice golf, which extends the short golfing season.

Tennis is popular, played on both indoor and outdoor courts. Horse riding is a favorite, particularly with young girls. You can swim in lakes, rivers, and the sea, and there are, of course, well-equipped swimming pools in all the major towns and cities.

As for spectator sports, ice hockey is number one. In 1995, when Finland became world champions for the first time, the whole country came to a standstill. The victory was all the sweeter because it was against the Swedes, the arch rivals, in Stockholm, and the coach of the Finnish team was Swedish. The Swedes had been so sure of their victory that they had prerecorded their victory song "Den glider in" ("The puck slides in"). These words were printed on thousands of T-shirts in Finland. It is said that Finnish self-esteem came of age on that day. Finns working in Sweden had been regarded as second-class citizens by some Swedes, but the morning after the victory many of those Finns held their heads up high for the first time. The victory could be compared to England's winning of the football World Cup in 1966.

Finland belongs to the world elite in ice hockey, and many young Finns have become millionaires in the National Hockey League in the U.S.A. and

Canada. Ice hockey is also played by women. It is the dream of many young Finns to make the NHL. This dream is stronger and more widely held than that of becoming a football star, though Finns are also present particularly in the English Premier League and in France and Germany. In international competition the Finnish national team has yet to qualify for a major tournament. The new international sporting hero is Kalle Palander, World Cup winner in alpine sports. *Pesäpallo*, or Finnish baseball, is a popular summer sport.

Finland has always produced fast rally drivers. Many cynics would say that this is easy and natural for the Finns as they get good practice on Finland's rough country roads. Formula 1 competitions keep Finns glued to their television sets, with names such as Häkkinen, Salo, and Räikkönen in the world elite.

Athletics in Finland are in decline. "The flying Finn," Paavo Nurmi, was on the shortlist for the sportsman of the twentieth century. Finnish cross-country skiers have been through doping scandals over the last few years. Traditionally this has been a strong sport for the Finns. Everybody interested in winter sports knows about the ski jumpers. You need to be very brave, if not foolhardy, to participate in this daredevil sport.

Finland is a country of mass sports events; this is truly sport for all. The women's 10-kilometer run in Helsinki, many marathons, rowing, relay running from Lapland to the south coast, the Finlandia ski event, and many more attract huge numbers of participants. It is common practice to enter these events with a team of colleagues. Exercise is enjoyed by all.

COUNTRY PURSUITS

Finland offers the perfect conditions for all kinds of outdoor pursuits. Trekking in Lapland is particularly enjoyable among the autumn colors. The facilities are good for staying overnight in wilderness huts. There is peace and quiet and solitude if you wish it. You can row on the lakes and canoe on the rivers. You can go whitewater rafting on the rapids. Telemark skiing in Lapland will test your endurance. Downhill skiing with plenty of *après-ski* is available in Lapland from December to May. There are an increasing number of adventure holidays and extreme sports on offer. Would you like to travel on an icebreaker, and finish off the adventure by swimming around it in a special survival suit?

And if sports don't interest you, you can go picking wild mushrooms and berries, or hunting for elks and capercaillie—a large kind of grouse.

THE COUNTRY CODE: EVERYMAN'S RIGHTS

The country code is a set of rules pertaining to acceptable behavior in the countryside.

You may walk, ski, or cycle freely in the country, except in gardens and in the immediate vicinity of homes and in fields or planted areas that could be damaged. You may stay or set up camp temporarily in the countryside at a reasonable distance from homes. You may pick wild berries, mushrooms, and flowers as long as they are not a protected species. You may fish with a rod and line, but for other kinds of fishing you need a license. You may row, sail, use a motorboat, swim, or wash in inland waters and the sea. You may walk, ski, drive a motor vehicle, or fish on frozen lakes, rivers, and the sea.

You may not damage property. You may not disturb the privacy of people's homes, for example by camping too near them or making too much noise. You may not disturb reindeer or game, or breeding birds, their nests, or their young. Tourists in Lapland often wait in their cars while reindeer bask on the warm asphalt road (giving good photo opportunities!).

You may not collect moss, lichen, or fallen trees from other people's property, except in an emergency. You may not drop or leave litter. You may not drive motor vehicles off the road without the permission of the landowner. You may not fish or hunt without the relevant permits.

TRAVELING

DRIVING

Finland is one of the mutually insured "green card" countries, and if you are driving yourself you will need an internationally recognized driver's license. Traffic drives on the right, and passes on the left. Seat belts are compulsory for the driver and all passengers, and all motor vehicles must use headlights at all times, regardless of the time of day or weather conditions.

Most traffic signs are similar to those in continental Europe. The expressway network is limited to the area around the main population centers. Roads are kept in good condition all year-round—snow clearing, sanding, and gritting of roads are efficient, with fleets of snowplows out in the early hours during the winter. Only very rarely, when there is an exceptionally heavy snowfall or a sudden frost, do roads become impassable. You need to be cautious and drive at slow speeds if you are not used to winter driving. Special winter tires are obligatory from December to February; studded tires are permitted from the beginning of November until after Easter and at other times when the weather conditions require their use.

The Finns are good drivers. They have produced several world champions in rally driving and in Formula 1, and they sometimes get carried away speeding on minor roads. There is a potential rally champion inside every Finnish driver. Speed restrictions are clearly marked, however, and fines for speeding are high.

Try Your Luck

When someone asked Ari Vatanen—the many times world rally champion, now a member of the European Parliament—what makes a good rally driver, he answered, "A heavy foot and an empty head!" If you want to give it a go, Ari Vatanen runs a rally-driving center in Northern Karelia.

You can find gas stations all over the country, and you can obtain free maps showing their locations. When traveling in remote areas, however, ensure that you have enough gas to complete your journey. Gas is unleaded; check details for the correct gas to use if you car is not converted for this. Service stations are usually open 7:00 a.m. to 9:00 p.m., Monday through Saturday, but shorter hours on Sundays. Most stations have automatic gas dispensers that take cash or credit cards and are open twenty-four hours a day.

Drinking and driving laws are very strict. Driving under the influence of alcohol or drugs is forbidden. The limit of alcohol allowed in the blood is 0.5 milligrams per milliliter, and infringement of this rule nearly always incurs a penalty in the form of a fine or imprisonment; 1.2 will incur a heavier penalty. When Finns go out to dinner or to a restaurant, they use taxis or public transportation to get home. Many people keep a personal alcohol meter to check that they are safe to drive after a party. Police frequently use roadblocks, especially on Saturday or Sunday mornings, to check drivers for alcohol. Heavy drinking the night before can mean that you are still over the limit the following morning. Young Finns take turns being the designated driver on evenings out—"I'll drive this Saturday, and you drive next Saturday"—people don't take risks.

One of the main hazards is the occurrence of animals such as elk and reindeer on the road, particularly at dusk and dawn. Watch out for warning road signs. A collision with one of these heavy animals can be very serious. In areas where the elk population is high, there are special fences to keep them off the road.

Be careful on summer evenings, as the low sun can seriously affect visibility. Most serious accidents are caused by careless passing. In case of an accident, call the general emergency number, 112, or local police on 10022. Police, ambulances, and rescue services are well-organized and efficient.

TAXIS

A taxi can be ordered ahead by telephoning 008 or a local number, available from the telephone directory, or can be hired right away from a taxi stand. Taxi stands are usually situated near major railway stations, shopping centers, airports, and, in smaller towns, by the main market square. Every taxi has a yellow sign (*taksi* or *taxi*) that, when illuminated, signifies that it is available for hire. The basic fare is 4.00 euros, and this rises gradually on a kilometer basis, as shown on the meter and depending on the number of passengers. At night—8:00 p.m. to 6:00 a.m.—on Saturdays from 4.00 p.m., and on Sundays, the basic fare is 6.20 euros. The waiting charge is 29.20 euros an hour.

Cameras have been installed in most taxis to protect the driver. Smoking is not allowed in taxis.

CYCLING

Most Finns own a bicycle and use it all year-round. There are cycle routes, and in towns there are special marked areas of pavements intended for cyclists.

Children usually cycle to school, and you see schoolyards with hundreds of bikes parked in special shelters. Citybikes in Helsinki are free for use around town, on payment of a small deposit, and you can return them to any of the twenty-five bicycle ports in the town. Helmets are recommended, and you can rent one from the Helsinki City tourist office. Other towns run similar schemes—check locally for details. If you want to take your bicycle on a bus or a train, you should check with the carrier; there may be a fee.

There is a network of cycling routes around Finland, marked by brown signs with a bicycle on them, or you can find special cycling maps that show the routes. Cycling is a good way to see the country in the summer. Most of Finland, with its gentle slopes, is ideal for cycling. In Lapland and in eastern Finland there are some demanding hills, and you need to be fit to manage them. The most popular area for cycling tours is the Åland Islands, where you can island-hop on ferries. Bicycle rental is widely available. Check local tourist offices for details. Remember a helmet, a cell phone, a raincoat, and some spares, including a pump, before you go on a longer trek. In-line skaters and roller skiers also use cycle routes.

Cyclists and pedestrians should watch out for snow falling from roofs in the spring. Slipping on icy roads and pavements results in some 40,000 injuries a year, so be careful, and wear shoes with a good grip, whether you are cycling or walking.

PUBLIC TRANSPORTATION

Public transportation is well-organized in Finland. Buses are the main form of local public transportation in all the towns. Helsinki is the only city in Finland with a metro network, and it also has trams. All public transportation timetables may be found on the Internet, and journey planners are also available.

Air Travel

Finland is well-connected to the rest of the world by air. Most major airlines fly to Helsinki, and some international carriers fly to Tampere, Turku, and Rovaniemi. There are also many charter flights, particularly to Lapland. You can travel by helicopter to Tallinn from Helsinki.

The domestic airline network is one of the densest in Europe. Helsinki-Vantaa airport has excellent facilities, including an e-service bar with full e-working facilities. The main operator on internal routes is Finnair, and there are some other, smaller carriers, including Air Botnia. Finnair has pioneered electronic ticketing, and its security and safety record is among the best in the world. There are various discounts available.

Trains

Passenger trains serve most of the country except northern Lapland. Most towns are connected by rail, but traveling east-west is more difficult than north-south. All the main railway lines lead to Helsinki. Some trains have special coaches for children, and some carry cars. All intercity trains have restaurants on board, and many have conference facilities. Sleeper services are available on all long-distance trains. Different types of ticket are available. There are also trains from Helsinki to Russia.

Coaches

Coach services cover more than 90 percent of public roads, and the timetables usually tie in with rail, air, and ship services. Smart cards may be used to pay for journeys operated by different companies. The coach stations are run by Matkahuolto.

Boats and Ferries

In addition to road travel, there are lake traffic routes in the summer, and boats to Sweden, Estonia, Poland, and Germany all year-round. Taking inland lake and river trips is a wonderful way to see the country. There is a coastal tourist route from Helsinki to Porvoo, and boats also go to some of the islands

on the coast of Helsinki. The Åland Islands have a connecting network of shipping routes and ferries. You can also travel from Lappeenranta through the Saimaa Canal to Viipuri, in Russia.

WHERE TO STAY

Hotels are generally of a good standard. Most have a sauna and many have a swimming pool as well. There are plenty of hotels to choose from, and special rates are often available, particularly on weekends, in the summer, and for groups. You can find listings on the Internet, or in guidebooks or tourist information centers.

Summer hotels are budget hotels operating in

university student hostels during the vacation, and are open from June 1 through August 31. Other types of accommodation include spas, youth hostels, holiday villages, log cabins, and campsites. There is also a wide choice of bed and breakfast accommodation and farmhouse vacations. You can also rent summerhouses and ski chalets. In Lapland, along the main hiking routes, you will find free shelters you can sleep in. In some of the lakeside towns, in the summer, accommodation is available on the steam cruisers.

HEALTH AND SECURITY

Finland has a good and efficient health service, with modern hospitals and health centers. The health-care system is a mixture of national and private care. Maternity care is among the best in the world, and the infant mortality rate is the lowest in the world. Dental care is good, but expensive. Although there are few serious health problems in Finland, the long dark winters can cause depression. Seasonal affective disorder (SAD) can be treated by special lights.

EU citizens have a right to health care under the EU agreements, and most Finnish doctors speak English. Most common remedies can be bought at supermarkets and pharmacies, where trained pharmacists also give advice on common ailments.

Finland is a very safe country. Crime rates are low. Bank robberies and burglaries are rare, though are unfortunately on the rise. Though pickpockets are few, it pays to be streetwise—they particularly target cell phones, especially at clubs and discotheques. The drug scene is minor compared to that of most other European countries.

CLOTHING

The clothes you take to Finland will, of course, depend on the time of your visit. Windows are triple-glazed, and it is always warm indoors.

The winter is cold, and you will need a warm, windproof coat, hat, and gloves. Most important of all is footwear. Make sure you have shoes with a good grip, because slipping on the ice and snow causes ten of thousands of broken ankles and wrists in Finland every year. If you are going on a snow safari in Lapland, the tour operators will supply you with appropriate clothing. At ski centers you can rent all the equipment you need.

The summer can be hot. Finns are becoming more and more fashion-conscious, though many spend most of their time in tracksuits. Prices are fairly competitive. Formal clothes are rarely worn, though people do dress up to go to theater and opera premieres.

chapter eight

BUSINESS BRIEFING

GETTING DOWN TO BUSINESS

Finnish businesspeople are highly educated, very
able, professional, and efficient. They usually
know exactly what they are doing, and work hard
to achieve their goals. They don't boast about it,
but just quietly get on with the business at hand.
The term "Protestant work ethic" could have been
invented to describe the way they work.

Finns are also imaginative and innovative. They
are good at foreign languages; indeed they have to
be, for nobody else speaks Finnish. They can be a
little melancholy, but this doesn't mean that they
are phlegmatic or slow—you need only look at
"their" sports: rally driving and Formula 1! These
sports require quick thinking and instant reactions.

Older Finns may have been reluctant to boast
about their achievements, but there is now a
younger generation of Finns who are no strangers
to appearing on reality television programs and
competing in pop idol contests. They are
brimming with self-confidence. The grandparents
of this new generation fought against the Russians

and lived through the hardships after the Second World War. The new generation was brought up by mothers who went out to work; they watch American sitcoms, eat at McDonald's, and have surfed the Internet for as long as they can remember. Their primary school class probably participated in global links through the Internet with schools all over the world. They are perfectionists at heart, like their grandparents, and expect perfection from their business partners, but they are products of the late twentieth century and feel completely at home in the global village.

Certain things have not changed. Once a Finn makes a promise, he keeps it. Silence is still part of the communication—you only ask questions if there is something you haven't understood. The propensity for innovation is inherited, and it is this skill that keeps companies like Nokia at the cutting edge. The young Finns are like fish in water with communications technology. They are self-assured and confident. Creativity has to work hand in hand with a good work-life balance. One of the latest urban developments to be built is Suurpelto, in Espoo, an area of high-tech modern urban living in a secure, family-oriented, rural setting with facilities for "wireless proximity working," as the Finns call it.

OFFICE STYLE AND ETIQUETTE

Generally, the atmosphere in a Finnish office is relaxed and informal. Dress is casual, and suits are worn for important meetings only. Finns are serious about getting down to business. They feel that working with others is not meant to be entertaining—you stick to the business at hand. They also assume that all the necessary information is given, and that there is therefore usually no need for any further questions or discussion.

People can be very frank with each other. If you don't like something, you say so. There are, however, certain points to remember.

In companies and organizations the formal pronoun "you," *te*, has given way to the informal address, *sinä*, but when meeting someone for the first time, it is better to be formal. Titles are usually not used. *Herra* (Mr.) or *rouva* (Mrs.) are used only if you don't know the person's first name.

It is polite to learn to pronounce the names of your Finnish clients and business contacts correctly. It is also a good idea from the business point of view! As most foreigners regard Finnish names as difficult or even impossible, Finns are used to mispronunciations, but if you get them right they will be delighted, and will really appreciate you as someone who has taken the trouble to say the names correctly.

When meeting a Finn for the first time, you should always shake hands. It is impolite not to do so. Then don't forget to shake hands again when you say good-bye. The handshake needs to be firm, but not a finger crusher. Once you know your business partner well, or if you meet frequently, it is not necessary to shake hands every time you meet, but do so if you haven't seen each other for a while. Always remember to greet people, and to introduce yourself, whether face-to-face or on the telephone, by using both your first name and your surname.

When you are introducing other people, remember to do it the correct way. Introduce a man to a woman, a younger person to an older one, a person alone to a party of people, and a junior staff member to a senior one.

Finnish Good Manners

A young Englishman, a finance analyst, told me a story about his first visit to Finland. He got into a taxi, and right away simply told the driver the address he wanted to go to. The driver turned around to him and, with a very strong Finnish accent, said in English, "Here in Finland, young man, we first say 'Good morning'!"

WHO'S WHO IN FINNISH BUSINESS

The most famous Finnish businessman in the world is the CEO of Nokia, Jorma Ollila. He and many of the other current prominent business leaders are due to retire by 2006, giving room for the next generation to come to the helm.

Although Finns do business in many areas, wood, paper, and electronics are the main fields of activity. Some of the fastest-developing areas are electrical and optical equipment and bio industry. Machinery, metals, chemicals, and transportation equipment are also important. Some of the most famous names around the world, in addition to Nokia, are Kone, the elevator and escalator manufacturers; Fortum, the energy and oil company (result of the merger of IVO and Neste); and Tietoenator, the information systems company (result of the merger of the Finnish Tieto and Swedish Enator companies), to mention just a few. Food packaging is another field of Finnish expertise.

The biggest export and import partners are Germany, Sweden, the U.K., the U.S.A., and Russia. Bioindustry and biotechnology are emerging as new fields. Bio Valley in Turku is a center for medicine, diagnostics, and functional or health-promoting foods. Oulu is a growing center for molecular and cell biology. Kuopio

Biocentre specializes in farming and pharmaceuticals. Finns pay great attention to the detail and design of their products, and there are many design companies. In textile and interior decoration Marimekko is a global brand led by the formidable Finnish businesswoman Kirsi Paakkanen, who turned the company around in the 1990s from the brink of bankruptcy to world fame. Finnish retail businesses are growing, particularly in Russia and the Baltic States.

COMMUNICATION STYLES
Finns are considered introverts, and Finnish businesspeople are no exception, but with increasing globalization and with many Finnish companies becoming international and doing business all over the world, the style is changing. The basic values have not changed, but the delivery is different.

The Finns are naturally modest, often quiet, and, if asked for a comment, will usually pause to think before replying. They usually think in silence, and there is very little overt body language, so you need to allow time for thought. Finns are comfortable with silence, even if you are not—so don't fidget, or it will be thought that you are not paying attention. They may give a measured, slow—sometimes painfully slow—response, and this is to give their words the gravity they are intended to have. In conversation it is considered bad manners to interrupt, though there are some regional differences. The more talkative Karelians and Savo people of the east are known to interrupt others, to the annoyance of their western Finnish counterparts. This is not easily forgiven. On the whole, Finns distrust people who talk a lot. Being matter-of-fact pays off with them, as they take things at face value.

The Finns are not always very diplomatic, because they state the truth of the matter without beating around the bush. Things are often stated as black or white. Sometimes this may sound very blunt and categorical, but this is not intentional—it is just the Finnish way.

To sum up, the Finns are by nature reluctant communicators, but they are learning to communicate. Nokia uses the slogan, "Nokia—connecting people." Nokia is the business leader in Finland in all senses of the word, and this goes also for communication styles. But there is often a hidden message. Nokia goes out of its way not to advertise the fact that it is Finnish, yet for a long time it ran an advertising campaign with two children dressed in yellow raincoats and wearing gum boots, flying a kite on a water's edge; the advertisement said: "We have come a long way from this." You need to be Finnish to understand the hidden message. Nokia started as a manufacturer of rubber tires and gum boots and went into electronics as a sideline . . . Nokia, like all Finns, is proud of its roots.

Finnish businesspeople usually speak good English, but it may be advisable, if you don't speak Finnish, to have the services of a translator or interpreter.

Reluctant Communicators

A Finnish schoolteacher asked an English colleague whether he had any problems with children speaking in the classroom. The Englishman said, "Yes, I can't get them to shut up!" The Finn remarked that her problem was getting the children to speak.

Finnish women are more communicative than men, as a rule, in all areas of life. There are a great many women in business in Finland, and their style is more communicative than that of their male counterparts. Many hold leading positions in Finnish companies, and sometimes the assumption of equality with men can be a problem, particularly when negotiating deals in the Far East and in some other cultures where women are not so prominent in public life.

PRESENTATIONS

Presentations are well-prepared, using all the latest electronic equipment. The delivery, however, is often bordering on monotonous. There is a great deal of factual information, the tone is usually serious, and the humor, if any, is often very dry. The knowledge of English may be good, but the Finnish accent can be difficult to understand. Very few Finns are so fluent that they do not need to read from their notes.

Don't try to do a hard sell on Finns—they won't trust you. Their sales philosophy is, "If it's good it will sell. You don't have to praise it." This attitude can be the downfall of a Finnish product abroad, and Finns need to develop their sales techniques.

If you are planning on using Finnish in your presentation, make sure you have practiced your pronunciation with a Finn. When people gather to listen, don't be surprised if they start filling up the seats from the back of the auditorium and leave the front rows empty. Reticence to occupy a prominent place is typically Finnish, and no reflection on you.

TEAMWORK

A Finn is naturally a loner. The pattern of early settlements in Finland was such that you would build your house on a hill near a waterway and your land would surround the house. Your neighbor would do the same, so the distance from one house to the other could be great. It is said the earlier settlers would be outraged if they saw wood shavings floating down the river past their house; this would inevitably mean that somebody had broken the rules and had settled too close to you. This may be a myth, but it certainly has more than a grain of truth. The Karelians were different: they lived communally, shared large houses, often had several wives each, and were traditionally traveling traders. There are distinct differences in attitudes to teamwork, although younger Finns are used to it, from the comprehensive education system.

The demands of modern business are such that, whether you like it or not, you will have to get used to teamwork and open offices. In fact team-building seminars and adventure weekends are big business in Finland.

LEADERSHIP AND DECISION MAKING

Decision making is usually a democratic process in a Finnish company. Quick decisions are followed by prompt actions, based on the principle that, if you are going to do something, you might as well get on with it.

Human rights and ecology issues are major factors in decision making. Doubts about any possible environmental concerns must be allayed. Finns have learned this the hard way. The cellulose and paper industry, back in the 1950s and 1960s, were big polluters, but there has been a  total turnaround in this respect. The forestry industry is a good model of sustainable development.

Women and men are equal. In the past, the leaders of Finnish business and industry were all men, and many boardroom matters were discussed during the famous sauna evenings. Firms still have saunas for entertaining clients, but this happens less now that there are so many female executives. These days you are more likely to be entertained by a round of golf or an evening at the opera.

Giving Gifts
When giving business gifts, make sure that you don't appear to be bribing anyone—bribery is unacceptable.

TIMING AND PUNCTUALITY

Finns are known for their punctuality and promptness. Eight o'clock means 8:00, not 8:05. If you have called in an electrician, and he says he will be at your house at 8:00 a.m., it would not be unusual for him to arrive at 7:30 a.m. or even earlier, and Finns would expect this. Deliveries are usually made as arranged, and payments are made promptly. Theatrical and musical performances start on time, and people do not keep you waiting. Of course, there are always exceptions, and there are some unpunctual Finns.

The twenty-four-hour clock is used for all official appointments and timetables. Finns also use the international week numbers. You hear people saying, "I will be busy in week 5, but I can meet you in week 6."

MEETINGS AND NEGOTIATIONS

The format of a meeting will be settled beforehand, and a formal meeting will have a chairman and an agenda. Finns don't like surprises—and they won't pull any surprises on you either.

Business negotiations are sometimes carried out at the company sauna or on the golf course. The sauna evenings can get very jolly, with lots of alcohol consumed. If you have been invited to lunch, the Finn will let you know if he wants it to be a working lunch. Alcohol is not usually consumed at business lunches these days—long, convivial lunches are a thing of the past. Finns don't usually drink during the working day, but they will make up for it at the bar afterward. Coffee is usually served at meetings.

HANDLING DISAGREEMENTS

Finns are very determined, and they hold strong opinions. Give a Finn time to think. If there is a justifiable cause for complaint, he will pursue his case. When there is a disagreement, you will be expected to negotiate your way out of it. There will be no emotional scene.

You need to remain firm, because the Finn will stick to his guns, but if you reason with him he will try to see your point of view. Finns are skilled negotiators, and are good at reaching a consensus. This is possibly reflected in the fact that there are many prominent Finnish peace negotiators in the world's trouble spots.

CONTRACTS

Once agreement has been reached, this is as good as a contract—there will be no surprises at a later stage. The Finns will rely on the agreement to hold, and there may be some delay in producing the paperwork or responding to letters. Finnish lawyers are very professional, however, and the contract will be drawn up meticulously.

chapter nine

COMMUNICATING

LANGUAGE

Finnish (*suomi*) is a Finno-Ugrian language. It is generally considered to be difficult, but in fact it is very logical, and almost mathematical in its rules of inflection and conjugation. English-speakers find the language quite hard to learn, but only because it has very little in common with English—though many English loan words are entering the language at the moment, via the Internet and computer language. Finns appreciate any effort on the part of a foreigner to speak Finnish. Finnish is one of the official languages of the European Union.

Both Finnish and Swedish (*svenska*) are official languages in Finland, with 93 percent of Finns speaking Finnish as their mother tongue, and 5.6 percent speaking Swedish as theirs. All official communications from the state administration and national institutions appear in both languages. Everybody in Finland learns the other domestic language at school. The south and southwest of Finland are the main Swedish-speaking areas together with the Åland Islands, which are 99 percent Swedish-speaking. Finnish is also spoken in northern Sweden along the river Tornio and by about 300,000 Finns living in Sweden. There are over a million Finns, or their descendants, outside Finland, many of them in the U.S.A., Canada, and Australia.

The Sami languages (*saami*) are spoken by about 1,700 people in Lapland. When traveling around Finland it is worth noting that the road signs are usually in both Finnish and Swedish, particularly in the south and the west of the country. The Finnish name is written first where the majority language locally is Finnish, and Swedish where it is Swedish. In the Sami-speaking areas in the north, signs also appear in the local Sami dialect. The language of the Roma and sign language are also recognized languages. Many dialects are spoken around Finland, but they are all mutually understandable to Finns. There is also a distinct difference between standard written language and spoken language.

Speaking English

All Finns learn English at school, and the younger ones have a good knowledge of it. It would be wrong to assume that you can always communicate in English, but you can usually find somebody who is willing to speak English if you need help. The accents can be quite strong. Finns often have a broad vocabulary, and they know their English grammar, but their pronunciation lets them down. Difficult English sounds for Finnish speakers are **th**, which often sounds like the soft *tö* coming out of a Finnish mouth. The different sibilant sounds, **s**, **sh**, **z**, and **j** are difficult for a Finn to differentiate between. If a Finn says, "Are you joking?" it sounds like, "Are you choking?" Misunderstandings do occur. Swedish-speaking Finns find English easier to speak, as do the Swedes, because English and Swedish are so closely related. The Finnish language does not have a gender. The pronoun *hän* means both "he" and "she," which can be confusing for an English speaker, for a Finn may use both these pronouns indiscriminately. It is also worth remembering, in business negotiations that include legal or technical language, that it may be advisable to use interpreters or official translators to avoid misunderstandings.

Finns can sometimes sound very bossy and abrupt when speaking English. It is common in Finnish to use the imperative, "Give!" "*Anna!*" "Take!" "*Ota!*" etc., as polite requests. "You want coffee?" is a direct translation from Finnish, and can sound a little odd to an English speaker, who would have expected, "Would you like some coffee?" Finns often use English swearwords; this can be disconcerting to an English speaker, but the swearing is not meant to be offensive. Finns also swear in Finnish, but not usually in polite company.

When using a directory or a dictionary you need to remember that Finnish has three letters that do not appear in English: the Swedish å (pronounced as the "o" in "hot"), the letter ä (pronounced as the "a" in "hat") and the letter ö (pronounced as the "er" in "herd"). They appear at the end of the alphabet. The letters *v* and *w* are interchangeable in Finnish.

SILENCE

The Finns respect silence, and are comfortable with it. Folk wisdom praises the virtue of silence as a sign of wisdom, and talkativeness as the sign of fools. In conversation there are moments of silence, when the Finn weighs up what has been said, before making his own contribution. In fact to answer immediately would signify lack of respect for the views of the previous speaker. Silence has been seriously studied as a form of communication by Finnish academics. Silence at the dinner table does not bother the Finns, but it can feel very awkward to someone from the English-speaking world, who is accustomed to keeping the conversation flowing.

Silence is a Precious Commodity

A British travel writer, trekking in Lapland with a Finnish guide, tells a story:

"We had walked for two days without seeing anybody. Then I saw someone in the distance, coming towards us, and really looked forward to exchanging views about the beauty of Lapland in the full glow of autumn colors. The man came closer and closer, passed us with barely a nod, and continued on his way. I turned to my guide to ask why we didn't stop to talk. The guide explained that this man would have come to the wilderness to enjoy the silence and to be alone, and that we had no right to disturb him."

BODY LANGUAGE

Finns are very serious and attentive when they are listening to you. They do not always smile a great deal, and there is very little overt body language, maybe a little nodding in agreement or interjections like "*hmm,*" "*jaa-a,*" "*juu,*" "*oho,*" "*voi voi,*" and "*aijjai.*" It is just as common to listen in silence. Some avoid eye contact because they are shy, but Finns are taught to look people in the eye, and it is considered good manners to do so.

The Finns are fond of making speeches. It is customary to make a speech at a birthday party, wedding, or other special occasion, or sometimes just to make an occasion special. There is a very marked difference after a few drinks—Finns definitely liven up and come out of their shells!

Handshakes are always expected when you greet someone for the first time, and also on departure. Young people do not usually shake hands among themselves, and when they are introduced they often just nod. The kiss on the cheek, continental-European-style, has made a big entrance in Finland. It is customary to hug close friends and family when you meet them after a long separation.

CONVERSATION

Finns enjoy exchanging views with others. Small talk doesn't come easily to them, but this doesn't mean that they don't like talking. The pace can be slow, and pauses are natural. Some Finns speak particularly slowly when they speak English. Silence, when considering what has been said, is expected and accepted. Responses can take a long time to come.

The most common topic of conversation is the weather. The Finnish climate provides plenty to talk about. A few remarks about the weather are exchanged at the start of most conversations, such as, "Have you heard the weather forecast?" Finns like to gossip like everybody else. Sports and TV programs are typical topics of conversation, as are politics and people in the public eye. A newcomer on the conversation front is complaining about EU bureaucracy.

Finns are taught not to interrupt someone who is speaking. Sometimes the slow pace of speech leads a foreign listener to think that the Finn has stopped, and he starts to speak, to the annoyance of the Finn who was only pausing to think. There are regional differences here: the Karelians and Savo people, both known for their chattiness, are more likely to interrupt each other than Finns from Häme or Pohjanmaa.

Finns also talk about money—at least other people's money—along with prices and wages; even illnesses and medication are common topics at the coffee table, and so is dieting.

Forms of Address

The Finnish language has the formal and informal address, like French and German. *Sinä* is the informal "you," and *te* is the formal. There used to be strict social rules about who could use the informal address to whom, and who was allowed to suggest being on first-name terms. Nowadays people are very informal. After being introduced you are usually invited to use first names, and it is perfectly acceptable to do so. If you do speak some Finnish, use the formal address until you are invited to do otherwise.

Finns very often avoid using direct address, if they are not sure whether to be formal or not. Finns do appreciate your learning to pronounce their names correctly. If you are not sure how to say a name, ask someone to help you. It is well worth the effort. When you introduce yourself, it is common to say your first name first and then your surname, but on a list of participants or guests it is common to have the surname first followed by the first name.

People are not as concerned with titles as they used to be, but if you want be deferential you can use titles like *tohtori*, doctor, or *professori*, professor. If you are doing business with Finns, you can always check the protocol with them—it is better to ask than to cause offense. The words for Mr. (*herra*), Mrs. (*rouva*), and Miss (*neiti*) are used only in very formal contexts or if you know only the person's surname. The press commonly refers to public figures just by their surnames or title and surname, such as Halonen or *Presidentti* Halonen when talking about the current president.

As Finnish has no gender marker, it is very difficult to see, from looking at a name, whether it is a man's or a woman's name, and therefore it is advisable to find out beforehand, if you need to know the gender, for instance, for practical arrangements for a meeting or a conference.

Most Finnish companies have a policy of using first names with all colleagues. Schoolchildren address their teachers by their first names. There has been a lot of discussion recently about the need to be more formal, particularly when dealing with German and French colleagues in the European institutions like the European Union.

Greetings

When you see someone first thing in the morning you say "*Hyvää huomenta*" ("Good morning"). Later on and through the day you can say "*Hyvää päivää*" ("Good day!"). In the evening you can say "*Hyvää iltaa*" ("Good evening"). All of these are answered by repeating the greeting back. When you leave you can say "*Näkemiin*" ("Good-bye").

The more informal greetings "*Hei!*" and "*Moi!*" both mean "Hello!" and can be used at any time of the day. "*Kiitos*" means "Thank you"; "*Olkaa hyvä*" means "Please," and is the formal and the plural; when talking to one person, whom you know well, you say "*Ole hyvä!*"

When you go into a shop or bar, you will be asked "*Mitä saa olla?*" ("What can I get you?" You can say "*Haluaisin . . . ,*" which means "I would like . . ." You can say your order in English and hope that you have a sales assistant who understands, or you can start by asking "*Puhutteko englantia?*" ("Do you speak English?"). If someone has gone out of their way to help you, you can say "*Kiitos avustanne!*" ("Thank you for your help.") Another useful phrase is "*Voisitteko sanoa . . .?*" ("Could you tell me . . .?")

HUMOR

Most Finns have a good sense of humor. Finnish is very rich and expressive and there are many words for different kinds of laughter. Much of the humor is based on playing with words. Finns like both crazy humor and subtle, dry humor, and are very good at cryptic self-irony. When life is tough, you need to laugh to get through it. Finns laugh at themselves—but they are not pleased if you laugh at them. They love telling jokes and funny stories. Sex is often a source of jokes, because it is still slightly taboo, and it is easier to deal with this by joking about it. Politicians are fair game.

The Minister's Wife

Ahti Karjalainen, the long-standing Finnish foreign minister, was a rich source of jokes about his poor pronunciation of English. He was staying at a New York hotel with his wife. At breakfast, Mrs. Karjalainen wanted some orange juice. He turned to the waiter and said:
"Excuse me, could you find some juice [pronounced as 'use'] for my wife?"

So what makes the Finns laugh? Popular TV programs include American sitcoms, such as *Frasier*, *Friends*, and *Sex and the City*, and many British comedy programs, such as *Mr. Bean* and *Yes, Prime Minister*. Risqué stories and jokes—particularly about the Swedes and the Russians—are relished, but their translation into English doesn't usually work. The annual publications of joke collections are always best-sellers. Joke e-mails and text messages are sent in the thousands.

The "Swedish Joke"

A Finn, a Swede, and a Norwegian were on a light aircraft. The plane was losing height, and the pilot said that someone had to jump out of the plane. The Norwegian and the Finn both said that the Swede should jump. "No, no, we can't do that," says the pilot. "We have to be fair. I'll ask you each a question, and the one who gets their answer wrong has to jump." He asks the Finn, "When did the Titanic sink?" He knows the answer. He asks the Norwegian, "How many people survived?" He tells him. The pilot turns to the Swede and says, "Now name the survivors in alphabetical order."

There are also a lot of jokes about the people of Laihia, who are renowned for their stinginess and penny-pinching. Helsinki people, and townspeople in general, tend to make fun of country people and their dialects.

WRITTEN COMMUNICATIONS

Most Finns in business know enough English to communicate by writing, but do not usually write as well as they speak. The Finns are not great letter writers, and written confirmation is not always sent: a verbal communication is often enough. Finns don't go back on their word.

Be aware that the language used in written communications may be very short and abrupt, and may appear arrogant. Only the essence of the message is written, and there are no flourishes. In fact, the short-and-to-the-point style of e-mail suits the Finns perfectly.

SERVICES

The Internet

The Internet is very widely used in Finland. All organizations and state institutions have their own Web sites. Internet banking is popular, and the security systems are good. Well over half a million Finns have Internet access at home, and a much larger number have access at school, university, or the workplace. It is also available in public libraries.

Telephone

To telephone abroad from Finland, first dial the international prefix 00, 990, 994, or 999, then the country code (without the general prefix 0), then the trunk code (without the general prefix 0 or to Spain 9), and then the subscriber's number.

To call Finland from abroad, first dial the international prefix from the country you are calling from, then 358 for Finland, then the trunk code without the 0, and then the subscriber's number.

For international directory inquiries, call 020 202. For inquiries about cell phone numbers, call 9800 83 53.

There are still some public telephones in Finland, and most of them are operated by telephone cards. But remember there are fewer and fewer public telephone booths in Finland because of the increasing number of cell phones; and many people now, particularly the young, no longer even subscribe to landlines. The Finnish telephone companies have been selling off telephone kiosks, and the ingenious Finns have put them to new uses. One telephone kiosk has been converted into a sauna!

Telephone directories and Yellow Pages can be found at post offices and hotels. They are also available online.

When a Finn answers the phone he usually gives his name. Many people have equipment displaying the caller details on their landline telephones.

Finns go to bed early because the working day starts early, and therefore you should not call anyone at home after 8:30 p.m. unless you have arranged to do so beforehand or you know the person you are calling very well.

Cell Phones

Finland is the promised land of cell phones. "*Matkapuhelin*" is the official Finnish word for a cell phone, but the common word in everyday language is "*kännykkä*," literally, "something that fits the palm of your hand." Finns take their cell phone everywhere they go. Children are often given their first cell 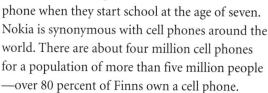 phone when they start school at the age of seven. Nokia is synonymous with cell phones around the world. There are about four million cell phones for a population of more than five million people —over 80 percent of Finns own a cell phone.

Text messaging is extremely popular with both young and old, and Finns send millions of text messages. Text messages can even be used as transport tickets, and you can use your mobile to buy a can of drink from a vending machine. You can use it as a remote control to switch on your sauna or the heating at your summer-house. It can be your camera and your games machine. Increasingly a cell phone is also a computer with full Internet connections. Many cell phones have compasses and homing devices, so you need never be lost! There are many cell phone operators in Finland, and the competition is fierce.

Mail

Finnish post offices, *posti*, are normally open Monday to Friday from 9:00 a.m. to 6:00 p.m., and closed on Saturdays and Sundays. There are some regional variations. There are also postal services available at some shops and service stations, and these often remain open later. The number of post offices have been cut radically recently.

Mailboxes in Finland are yellow, and they are usually emptied daily. Personal mail collection (poste restante) services are available at main post offices only. (In Helsinki the Main Post Office is in Elielinaukio, near the main railway station.)

Information on postal services and current rates is available at post offices or online. Stamps, *postimerkki*, can also be bought in bookshops, R-kiosks, stations, and hotels, and from stamp machines.

Mail is delivered to mailboxes outside Finnish houses. There is one delivery on each weekday, and no deliveries on Saturday or Sunday. There is first-class and second-class mail. Newspapers are also delivered to the mailboxes. In apartment blocks the mail is delivered to the apartment or to indoor mailboxes. In the summer many Finns have their mail diverted to their summerhouses.

CONCLUSION

The Finns are a resilient and very independent people. Very much at home in the global village, they have their roots firmly in Finnish soil. Even though most Finns now live in cities, their links to the countryside and to nature are strong. The landscape is beautiful, and the people appreciate the beauty throughout the seasons, which make the country a different experience at each time of the year. The street cafés in the summer give way to snow and ice in the winter, but there are always ways to enjoy the country.

The Finns and their language have survived

through centuries of foreign rule. Both the language and the people have absorbed foreign influences while retaining a strong national identity. The Finnish identity has been forged from the West by Western European culture and the Church, and from the East by the Orthodox Church.

From the Roman historian Tacitus to the intrepid Mrs. Alex Tweedie, who traveled "Through Finland in carts" at the start of the twentieth century, the foreign traveler has been fascinated with the "Ultima Thule," the far north.

There is much to be enjoyed in Finland. Business is thriving. The music scene is excellent. Arts and design permeate the whole society. The

architecture varies from medieval stone churches to modern icons of cutting-edge design. Then there is the great outdoors, with sports from fishing to golf, from ski marathons to canoeing the rivers. You can take your pick.

Finland is very much part of Europe, but is still one of the most remote, spacious, and beautiful corners of the continent. Its land and people are well worth exploring.

Further Reading

Aho, Kalevi, Pekka Jalkanen, Erkki Salmenhaara, and Keijo Virtamo. *Finnish Music.* Helsinki: Otava, 1996.

Arter, David. *Politics and Policy-Making in Finland.* Brighton: Wheatsheaf Books/New York: St.Martin's Press, 1987.

Bell, Marjatta, and Marjatta Hietala. *Helsinki—the Innovative City—Historical Perspectives.* Helsinki: Finnish Literature Society & City of Helsinki Urban Facts, 2002.

Castells, Manuel, and Pekka Himanka. *The Information Society and the Welfare Society. The Finnish Model.* Oxford: Oxford University Press, 2002.

Engman, Max, and David Kirby (editors). *Finland—People Nation State.* London: Hurst & Company, 1989; Bloomington and Indianapolis: Indiana University Press, 1989.

Hautala, Hannu, Lasse Lehtinen, and Lassi Rautiainen. *My Forest—Full of Life.* Helsinki: Edita, 2002

Jakobson, Max. *Finland: Myth and Reality.* Helsinki: Otava, 1987.

Jutila, Osmo, Seppo Hentilä, and Jukka Nevakivi. *From Grand Duchy to a Modern State—A Political History of Finland since 1809.* London: Hurst & Company, 1995.

Koivisto, Mauno. *Foreign Policy Standpoints 1982–1992—Finland and Europe.* Salcombe: Aidan Ellis, 1992.

Laitinen, Kai. *Vision.* Helsinki: Finnish Society of Crafts and Design, 1966.

Lipponen, Päivi, and Päivi Setälä (editors). *Women in Finland.* Helsinki: Otava, 1999.

Mead, W. R., and Helmer Smeds. *Winter in Finland.* London: Hugh Evelyn, 1967.

Swallow, Deborah. *Culture Shock! Finland.* Portland, Oregon: Graphic Arts Center Publishing, 2001/London: Kuperard, 2003.

Tiainen, Jussi. *New Finnish Architecture.* Helsinki: The Finnish Building Centre, 1997.

Making Connections Finland—Gateway to Northern Europe. Helsinki: The Finnish Foreign Trade Association, 1994.

The Finnish Landscape (collection of essays). Helsinki: The National Library of Finland, 2002.

Index

Acknowledgment

I would like to dedicate this book to my parents,
Tyyne and Arttu Kauppinen.